Success Is Possible

Success Is Possible

Creating a Mentoring Program to Support K–12 Teachers

Stefanie R. Sorbet
Patricia Kohler-Evans

ROWMAN & LITTLEFIELD
Lanham • Boulder • New York • London

Published by Rowman & Littlefield
An imprint of The Rowman & Littlefield Publishing Group, Inc.
4501 Forbes Boulevard, Suite 200, Lanham, Maryland 20706
www.rowman.com

6 Tinworth Street, London SE11 5AL

Copyright © 2019 by Stefanie R. Sorbet and Patricia Kohler-Evans

All rights reserved. No part of this book may be reproduced in any form or by any electronic or mechanical means, including information storage and retrieval systems, without written permission from the publisher, except by a reviewer who may quote passages in a review.

British Library Cataloguing in Publication Information Available

Library of Congress Cataloging-in-Publication Data

Names: Sorbet, Stefanie R., 1975- author. | Kohler-Evans, Patricia, 1951-, author.
Title: Success is possible : creating a mentoring program to support K-12 teachers / Stefanie R. Sorbet, Patricia Kohler-Evans.
Description: Lanham, Maryland : Rowman & Littlefield, [2019] | Includes bibliographical references.
Identifiers: LCCN 2019013128 (print) | LCCN 2019021863 (ebook) | ISBN 9781475849530 (electronic) | ISBN 9781475849394 (cloth) | ISBN 9781475849400 (pbk.)
Subjects: LCSH: Mentoring in education. | Teachers—Professional relationships. | Teacher turnover—Prevention.
Classification: LCC LB1731.4 (ebook) | LCC LB1731.4 .S57 2019 (print) | DDC 371.1—dc23
LC record available at https://lccn.loc.gov/2019013128

Contents

Preface	vii
Acknowledgments	ix
Introduction	xi
1 Send Help Quick	1
2 Research: The Backstory	9
3 Roles: Team of Leaders	17
4 Navigating through Change	29
5 Addressing Concerns for Beginning Teachers	35
6 Addressing Concerns for Mentor Teachers	49
7 Addressing Concerns for Curriculum Coaches	63
8 Addressing Concerns for Peer Buddies	75
9 Professional Development Resources	83
10 Beginning Teacher Retreat and Induction	93
11 Guiding and Documenting Implementation	97
12 Timeline of Implementation	103
References	107
About the Authors	109

Preface

In my office, hanging in front of the windows, is a stained glass piece, crafted by my husband. It carries a simple yet powerful message: "*Let Your Life Speak.*" I hung the piece above my desk, and it is a daily reminder to seek out deeper meaning from these four simple words. I am aware that my life will invariably speak regardless of the ways I hope it does. My actions will herald my authentic self, whether that is the self I want to portray or the one who shows up on my worst days.

What I continue to draw from these profound words each day is how very much I want to have *my* life speak in affirming, loving, compassionate, and transformational ways. I want to instill a passion for personal growth; a love for the profession of teaching; a deep desire to embrace every child, especially those who struggle; and a tenacity that gently prods each new teacher candidate to seek out and find the best answers for his or her own students. If I am able to accomplish even a fraction of this, I know my life will have spoken well.

The journey to this place has been peppered along the way by countless individuals whose lives have touched mine in unimaginable ways. So, where to begin? I was born 67 years ago, in New York, the first daughter of a teacher and civil engineer. My mom was my first mentor and teacher, and she taught me well. From her I learned to love books and music, and to say my prayers every night.

Mom taught me to practice my scales on the piano and to be kind to grasshoppers and not to pull their legs off. She taught me not to hit my younger sisters, but rather to help care for them. She would bend gently from the waist, clasp her hands behind her back, and share great wisdom with me.

In the fall of my sixth year, my neighbors adopted a child who had been brought up in the worst conditions. I grew up in Little Rock during the

Central High Crisis, and my next-door neighbors, the Woods, adopted a little girl whose name was Catherine. Catherine was my playmate and best friend. Her new parents shepherded me and helped mentor me as I learned to play with someone vastly different from myself. This family taught me about appreciating differences and celebrating diversity.

Just a few years later, I found myself under the care and concern of another amazing individual, my sixth-grade teacher, Helen Ruth Smith. Miss Smith saw in me a shy, introverted, fearful child, and under her watchful eye, I was mentored once again. This remarkable woman introduced me to self-confidence and self-determination. She gently took me under her wing, and she changed the course of my life with her guidance. She was fierce and passionate, and I learned to roar while being gentle.

All along the way, these remarkable individuals, my mother, my neighbors, and my teacher, gently guided and mentored me with their deep desire to positively impact another's life. Gratefully, I acknowledge their gifts. It is no small wonder that, in this day when teachers are leaving the profession almost before they acclimate to the school building, one of the greatest gifts one might bestow is sharing a journey while helping pave the uncertain path invariably presented by a new classroom full of children.

Our teachers are often the best advocates and champions our children have, and it is imperative that we not lose them! How can we best provide the support and caring that new teachers crave? The answer is simple: by giving them our best wisdom and nurturing them so that they survive and thrive. When teachers are cared for, understood, and led with kindness, they provide care, understanding, and leadership for the children whose futures depend on them.

—Patricia Kohler-Evans

Acknowledgments

This book is dedicated to the many beginning teachers who enter the teaching profession so that they can make a difference but are not afforded a network of support to accomplish this goal.

To all of our family and friends, our greatest mentors, who have empowered and motivated us to create this guide to sustain the teaching profession, we thank you. We are grateful for your presence and your continued support.

Introduction

Success Is Possible: Creating a Mentoring Program to Support K–12 Teachers provides the guidance school administrators need to welcome, care for, and nurture new teachers. The book is divided into 12 chapters. Chapter 1 provides a background and explains the need for mentoring programs within schools targeted at building relationships between the new teacher and a mentor. Chapter 2 gives a broad overview of research supporting the idea of implementing mentoring programs within schools.

Chapter 3 clearly defines the roles of the beginning teacher, mentor, coach, and peer buddy who make up the collaboration team and work together to aid in the assistance and support of the beginning teacher throughout the first three years of teaching. Chapter 4 provides recommendations for the appropriate setting and sample in which this mentoring program should be implemented, including a timeline displaying all of the requirements for the mentor, administrator, coach, and peer buddy as well as the beginning teacher for the first through third years of teaching.

Chapters 5 and 6 address key concerns for the beginning teacher and the mentor teacher, respectively. Chapters 7 and 8 address key concerns for the coach and peer buddy, respectively. Chapter 9 highlights professional development topics of trainings for new teachers as well as a timeline showing how these may be prioritized within the first year of teaching.

Chapter 10 suggests ideas and topics for new teacher induction and a retreat designed to encourage and support beginning teachers as well as veteran or mentor teachers. Chapter 11 assists administrators who are implementing a mentoring program and utilizing this book to guide and document implementation using several questionnaires to measure and track the change process to higher teacher retention.

Chapter 12 provides tools to assist with measuring the progress of program implementation, including survey instruments. These instruments are designed to measure growth within the first year of implementation as well as identify any future changes to be made based on the voiced needs of the new teachers involved.

It is only when we embrace each novice teacher with all the wisdom and knowledge of the experienced and seasoned teacher that we ensure that the most precious lives of all receive an outstanding foundation on which to build a glorious future. Use this book as a constant companion to help through the critical first few years of the novice teacher's experience to nurture and support for the long-distance haul. By doing so, the next generation of mentor teachers is already being cultivated.

Chapter One

Send Help Quick

THE PROBLEM

Teacher retention is one of the most pressing issues in education. In well over 100,000 classrooms, America's children are served by underqualified teachers. The nation is in a teacher shortage crisis, and children pay the consequences when their instructional needs are not fully addressed.

How can we raise an educated populace who will become our next generation of doctors, business owners, scientists, or even teachers without high-quality instruction by fully qualified teachers? More importantly, how can we provide the support needed to retain those who have invested their time and effort into answering the call to teach our nation's youth?

Nationally, teacher attrition and retention cost the country billions of dollars each year (Darling-Hammond, 2006). In a recent report, 90% of open teaching positions were created by teachers leaving the profession. This is an alarming circumstance. Teacher turnover rates are high and new teacher support is needed so districts do not have the constant task of filling vacancies each year. According to Ingersoll and Smith (2003), 40–50% of teachers leave the profession within the first five years.

Teacher retention is of utmost importance during a time when teachers are highly criticized and blamed for so many of the uncontrollable stimuli that children face. Teachers who leave the profession cite a lack of administrative support, working with low salaries, dissatisfaction with accountability pressures, poor working conditions, and limited options for advancement as reasons for leaving.

Implementing support for beginning teachers in their first three years will guarantee help and assistance during the difficult time of adjusting to a new career. Mentoring programs are critical when teachers are leaving the profession as quickly as they are leaving.

In Sorbet's (2018) study, the results indicate mentoring may be a way to engage new and veteran teachers. Mentoring provides a "challenge" for mentors to mold mentees while "reflecting" on the process and improving themselves. Both mentors and mentees "grow" in the relationship as they reflect on the experiences through teaching and observing each other.

By supporting beginning teachers and encouraging them to remain in the profession long enough to feel confident at their job, school districts might begin to feel a shift of focus from teacher evaluation and remediation of teachers to a community of support and professional development for teachers both beginning and veteran.

If districts take time to invest in their beginning teachers as they form bonds and a community within their schools from the start, then teachers will be more likely to continue within the profession feeling that sense of support and achievement. When educational leaders encourage veteran teachers to serve as mentors to new teachers, the benefits are well worth the effort. Intrinsic motivation, increased commitment to the future, and professional development to create strong teacher leaders are only a few of the myriad possibilities.

Districts must support beginning teachers so they can become strong leaders within schools and, in turn, mentor other beginning teachers based on personal, quality experiences. This effect can push forward as new teachers are mentored, grow into leaders, and mentor others, providing an ongoing network of support.

THE SOLUTION

By creating mentoring programs to support mentors and mentees, districts motivate and encourage community and relationships between veteran and new teachers, which also encourages both to remain within the profession. School districts will begin to feel a change of focus from teacher evaluation and remediation of teachers to more of a community of support with continued professional development for both beginning and veteran teachers.

Mentoring relationships encourage and support the new teacher or mentee to grow while providing an opportunity for the veteran teacher or mentor to be challenged through strengthening and reflecting on his or her own teaching abilities. Veteran and new teachers are constantly in need of support to face new challenges.

Mentoring programs strengthen faculty relationships within school communities while increasing teachers' motivation and drive to remain in the profession. If teachers are appreciated, supported, and intrinsically motivated, they will want to be in schools, and they will remain.

As educational leaders search for an opportunity to motivate the best and strongest veteran teachers while supporting new teachers to be successful in the profession, establishing a mentoring program is an effective way to accomplish the task. During these tough educational times where funding is scarce, leaders can foster community and relationships among faculty through mentoring programs within their schools. These mentoring relationships will serve as their own prescribed in-house professional development intervention servicing both new and veteran teachers.

Educational leaders and their schools benefit from research that determines the motivational factors of the mentor and the mentee within a mentoring relationship and how they compare. Educational leaders will find it important to discover which reciprocal benefits are experienced within a mentoring relationship and to determine how to best utilize mentoring as a method for cultivating these benefits through building relationships. These efforts will build community and raise teacher retention rates within their school districts.

THE BENEFITS FOR MENTORS AND MENTEES

When addressing who really benefits in a mentoring relationship, the mentor or the mentee, the answer is both. A recent study of mentors and mentees provides evidence that challenge and reflection intrinsically drive mentors while challenge and growth drive the mentees. Mentors are motivated due to the challenge of taking on a new teacher, showing him or her best practices, and reflecting on their own teaching skills and ways to improve. The mentee is motivated by the challenge of a new teacher position and the growth experienced throughout the relationship with a mentor teacher (Sorbet, 2018).

Mentoring relationships are routes for gaining the professional and personal skills that are necessary for working in collaborative work environments (Kochran & Smith, 2000). Mentoring relationships that provide reciprocal trust and openness can enhance the further development of both the mentor and new teacher's personal and professional collaborative work skills (Kochran & Smith, 2000).

With veteran and beginning teachers working together, beginning teachers gain experience in the field with a support system for them to lean on. This system fosters a community support network in which beginning teachers feel supported and have quality examples to refer to while sustaining focus and optimism throughout the process.

Mentors engage in mentoring relationships as a means of meeting their intrinsic motivation in the areas of self-reflection, improving overall teaching abilities, and self-actualization. Mentoring promotes self-analysis of the mentor's teaching practices, including teaching students, learning, and teaching as their own career (Ganser, 1997).

The mentors take on new teachers as a means for fulfilling their need to grow professionally. They know that through assisting and collaborating with the new teachers, they will essentially grow in their professional career. The mentor teachers grow in socialization as they increase in collaboration and assistance provided to the new teachers (Olson, 2008). The mentors also grow in their skill set in the areas of listening before reacting and providing nonjudgmental feedback to the new teachers (Olson, 2008).

Such research as this provides educational leaders the idea that fostering reciprocal relationships between the mentor and the mentee can be a means of motivating teachers through instilling reflection, growth, and challenge. If a mentor and a mentee are engaged within a mentoring relationship, then reciprocal intrinsic motivation develops from within.

Intrinsically motivating mentors and mentees, specifically in the areas of reflection, growth, and challenge, can improve job satisfaction. Improving job satisfaction in both new and veteran teachers can be the driving force behind new and veteran teacher retention.

Educational leaders can look to mentoring programs that foster relationships to increase intrinsic motivation by providing the challenge that veteran teachers or mentors long for, the growth necessary for new teachers or mentees to become successful in the profession, and the reflection necessary to adjust and improve all involved throughout their career.

By creating mentoring programs to support mentors and mentees, districts motivate and encourage community and relationships between veteran and new teachers, which also encourages both to remain within the profession (Sorbet, 2018). Fostering mentoring programs within districts and encouraging supportive, mentoring relationships within the school building can start to increase intrinsic motivation while improving new and veteran teacher retention.

School districts can begin to feel a shift of focus from teacher evaluation and remediation of teachers to more of a community of support and continuing professional development for beginning and veteran teachers. If educational leaders take time to invest in their beginning teachers, helping them to form bonds and a community within their schools through engaging as mentees within mentoring relationships, then beginning teachers may become more motivated to continue in the profession.

THE BENEFITS FOR STUDENTS

Novice and veteran teachers are not the only ones to benefit from a mentoring program. Educational leaders should understand that allowing experienced teachers to mentor new teachers could ultimately provide benefits to the students within both the mentors' and mentees' classrooms, thus improving the overall school organization (Huling & Resta, 2001).

Mentoring promotes self-analysis of the mentor's own teaching practices, including teaching students, learning, and teaching as their own career (Ganser, 1997). The mentor assists and supports the new teacher through the day-to-day routines of planning, instructing, assessing, and intervening with students as they reflect on current teaching practices.

The mentor teachers grow in task development through improving their ability to better assess student learning, implement teaching strategies, and heighten their use of questioning methods (Olson, 2008). The mentors spend their time modeling and providing quality examples of teaching pedagogy and methodology for the new teachers and become stronger teachers while refining practice through careful planning and execution of well-thought-out lessons.

The mentors also observe the new teachers as they take advice from the mentors and implement teaching strategies in daily lessons. The mentors then evaluate the methodology of teaching to determine if these are still the most current best practices for individual students.

The mentors become reflective practitioners by reflecting on current practices and ideas that are currently being used in the classroom and assessing if these practices are appropriate enough to meet the needs of the students in their classroom. The mentor teacher continues to become more reflective in practice as they encourage the new teachers to implement the mentors' own methods and strategies into the new teachers' methodology.

The new teachers grow professionally in this process as they lean on the mentors to develop as professionals. The new teachers show growth over time and slowly arrive at the stage where they are interacting and sharing as partners with other teachers within their grade levels. When new teachers learn how to communicate in professional learning communities with others as they act as part of a team, students are the ultimate beneficiaries.

Through mentoring, the veteran teachers better understand their own personal strengths and challenges as teachers and seek new professional development opportunities to improve (Olson, 2008). The mentees become more reflective practitioners in that as they teach, the mentor teachers provide feedback and assist the mentees in the areas of planning, curriculum design, organization, management, and overall instruction of students.

The mentees reflect on teachings and determine what worked well and what should be adjusted. As the mentor teachers model and demonstrate pedagogy and methods of teaching to new teachers, the mentors reflect and determine if their current methodology is working in the classroom as they observe the new teachers.

As educational leaders decide where to spend funds for staff development, they can begin to look to mentoring programs not just for professional development of beginning teachers, but also for self-growth experiences for mentor teachers (Huling & Resta, 2001). According to Huling and Resta,

> mentors can exert substantially greater influence on the school organization than novices, the benefits mentors derive from mentoring may be of equal, or even greater, importance than those experienced by novice teachers. (p. 4)

The benefits to establishing a mentorship program are endless. New teachers, veteran teachers, and ultimately the students are all recipients of a carefully constructed, well-developed, and purposefully implemented mentoring program.

MODEL FOR CHANGE

A common misconception of administrators and leaders is that once an innovation is introduced and members of the organization are trained, the change is then put into action. We know that change is messy, has many layers, and takes time. Positive change occurs over time, and organizational members experience a variety of needs as they go through the change process.

As with any innovation, successfully implementing a mentoring program takes considerable time and understanding of the unique concerns that novice and veteran teachers bring to the classroom. It is only through a deep appreciation of each educator's perspectives that an attentive administrator can fully address individual concerns.

One model for change implementation that has hooked education leaders for decades is the Concerns-Based Adoption Model, or CBAM. The authors suggest using CBAM to implement change (Hord, Rutherford, Huling-Austin, & Hall, 1987). It is important to consider CBAM when implementing change within an organization as a way to acknowledge these needs throughout the change process (Hall & Hord, 2006).

CBAM applies attention to the concerns of the individuals involved in or experiencing the change. CBAM helps administrators and leaders look at the implemented change through the lens of the multiple perspectives of all involved with carrying out the change.

There is such a great need for leaders of an organization to utilize such an approach when implementing change. The administration within an organization must recognize there may be resistance to any change that will be brought to an organization. In the case of creating mentoring partnerships between new and veteran teachers, everyone's concerns should be factored in prior to implementation of a new mentoring program.

New teachers are faced with guidelines, processes, developing lesson plans, managing a classroom, parental relationships, learning the established ways of doing the work, and a host of other challenges. These are just a few of the myriad issues faced during the first year of the teaching profession.

Veteran teachers may have different concerns than those of new teachers. Veteran teachers may also feel overwhelmed with time constraints of their own and not want to take on a mentee. Veteran teachers may show resentment toward a new mentoring program in that they did not have such a supportive network when they were beginning teachers. The administration should recognize and address these concerns and reassure faculty members that the change being implemented will not only assist beginning teachers but will also provide an opportunity for veteran teachers to move into leadership roles.

Readers of this book will be taken through each of the seven stages of concern for the beginning teacher, mentor teacher, coach, and peer buddy through full implementation. Throughout the book, readers are provided information for all involved in the implementation process of change utilizing CBAM paired with a timeline to show the expectations of all parties. Additional timelines and long-range plans are provided to assist administrators through the implementation process.

ROADMAP FOR CHANGE

This book is designed to guide district and school administrators who see supporting beginning teachers as relevant to today's teaching profession. Content presented here provides guidance for the creation of a network of support targeting all areas of the new teachers' needs while simultaneously developing a support system for them to rely on to access the necessary materials and knowledge needed to be successful. This guide provides administrators the tools necessary to transition new teachers into their first year of the profession.

The roles of the collaboration team and all members of the team supporting the beginning teacher will be explored. Principals and administrators will become aware of the value in investing in beginning teachers so that time and money will not be spent for their remediation later. Teacher retention will be stressed to the administrators and faculty involved. It is of utmost importance to encourage and support beginning teachers through the utilization of the knowledge and expertise of the veteran teachers who serve as mentors for new teachers.

Educational leaders should look to mentoring relationships and programming to support the development of future leaders by providing the challenge that veteran teachers or mentors long for, the growth necessary for new teachers or mentees to become successful in the profession, and the reflection necessary to adjust and improve throughout their career. Fostering mentoring programs within districts and encouraging supportive, mentoring relationships within school buildings can start to increase intrinsic motivation while improving new and veteran teacher retention.

This may result in a roll-forward effect, with those who were mentored making the decision to become mentors themselves based on their own personal, quality experiences as part of the mentoring process. This can result in supporting the next generation of new teachers (Sorbet, 2018).

If teacher retention is of great concern because it is costly to school districts and impacts student achievement, then it is imperative to all educational leaders to address this compounding issue to best move school districts forward. Teachers need support, and mentoring programs are the key to rekindling the intrinsic motivation of veteran teachers while supporting and modeling that same motivation for new teachers. Mentoring relationships can foster intrinsic motivation within the mentor and the mentee while creating a cycle of reflection, growth, and challenge that can be carried on through the years.

By fostering mentoring programs that support and motivate both new and veteran teachers, educational leaders will begin to experience a powerful sense of community within the school building as well as decreased teacher exodus. When all teachers are valued in their profession, they will fervently educate our youth and continue the cycle of impact for tomorrow's educators.

KEY POINTS

Teacher retention is one of the most pressing issues in education. Teachers who leave the profession cite many reasons for leaving. Implementing support for beginning teachers in their first three years provides help and assistance during the difficult time of adjusting to a new career. Mentoring programs are critical when teachers are leaving the profession as quickly as they are leaving. A mentoring program benefits both the mentor and the mentee.

Chapter Two

Research

The Backstory

The number of teachers who enter and exit the field of education within the first five years is an alarming 40–50% (Ingersoll, 2012). What is more startling is that teachers leaving the profession increased by 28%, from 13.2% in 1991–1992 to 16.9% in 2004–2005. First-year public school teacher attrition rates rose from 21.4% to 28.5% from 1988 to 2004 (Ingersoll & Merrill, 2010).

It is critical that educational leaders look toward mentoring programs that foster reciprocal relationships between the beginning teacher (mentee) and the veteran teacher (mentor) as a means of improving overall teacher retention. Schools with mentoring services show higher new teacher retention rates than those schools in which such services are not provided to new teachers (Di Carlo, 2015). Mentoring promotes self-analysis of the mentor's own teaching practices as they relate to students, learning, and teaching as their own career (Ganser, 1997).

When examining the potential offered through mentoring while contemplating the serious nature of the mass exodus from the profession, Sorbet (2018) sought to answer critical questions in an effort to explore elements of highly effective mentoring programs and determine if mentors engaged in mentoring relationships as a means of meeting their intrinsic motivation in the areas of self-reflection, improving overall teaching abilities, and self-actualization.

Sorbet began her search for answers to questions posed about mentors' needs by examining Maslow's *Hierarchy of Needs* (1943). Maslow's hierarchy identifies five levels, which include (a) physiological needs, (b) safety, (c) belonging, (d) esteem, and (e) self-actualization. Sorbet adapted Maslow's work and created the *Hierarchy of Teachers' Needs* to include parallel levels of need: (a) basic needs including organizational skills and classroom management, (b) feeling comfortable and safe, (c) interacting with others, (d) feelings of success, and (e) self-actualization. The Hierarchy of Teachers' Needs is displayed in Figure 2.1.

New teachers or mentees steadily climb through the extrinsic factors as they gain experience in the teaching profession. The mentees gain experience and slowly arrive at the stage or level where they are interacting and sharing among other teachers within their grade level as the new teachers learn how to communicate in professional learning communities and with others as they act as part of a team.

During this process, veteran teachers serving as mentors have feelings of success when others seek their advice, demonstrating recognition of their hard work. These more experienced teachers are then approached to mentor other teachers. The mentor teachers reach the final and highest level of the chart when they are self-actualized, which is very similar to the highest level of Maslow's (1943) Hierarchy of Needs. This level represents the selfless leader who is willing to assist and support others in the profession, driven by intrinsic motivation and satisfaction, and willing to simply contribute to the field of education.

Sorbet (2018) analyzed the possible relationship between Maslow's Hierarchy of Needs (1943), Hertzberg's *Two-Factor Theory of Motivation* (1959), and Frase's (1989) connection of these two theories in education. As teachers move upward through their individual teacher needs, they are driven by both intrinsic and extrinsic motivation through reflection, growth, and challenge.

Frederick Herzberg, a former professor of management at the University of Utah, focused his research on the main sources of employee motivation in the workplace. Herzberg developed the Two-Factor Theory of hygiene and motivator factors. As further explained by Dudovskiy (2013), Herzberg discovered the motivating factors that affected people's performance in the workplace. Dudovskiy's (2013) theory detailed the hygiene or extrinsic motivators and the motivator or intrinsic factors that drive people in the workplace to address job satisfaction and rewards.

Herzberg's intrinsic motivators satisfy the need for self-actualization (Stello, 2011). Self-actualization sits at the highest part of Maslow's Hierarchy of Needs chart and the Hierarchy of Teachers' Needs chart as well (Sorbet, 2018). These intrinsic motivators include aspects of the status, recognition, wages, achievement, responsibility, and advancement or growth (Herzberg, 1966). Intrinsic motivators include status because the motivation is present in the way others perceive you.

Herzberg's extrinsic or hygiene factors are related to the completion of the job (Stello, 2011). These factors include (a) salaries, (b) wages, (c) bene-

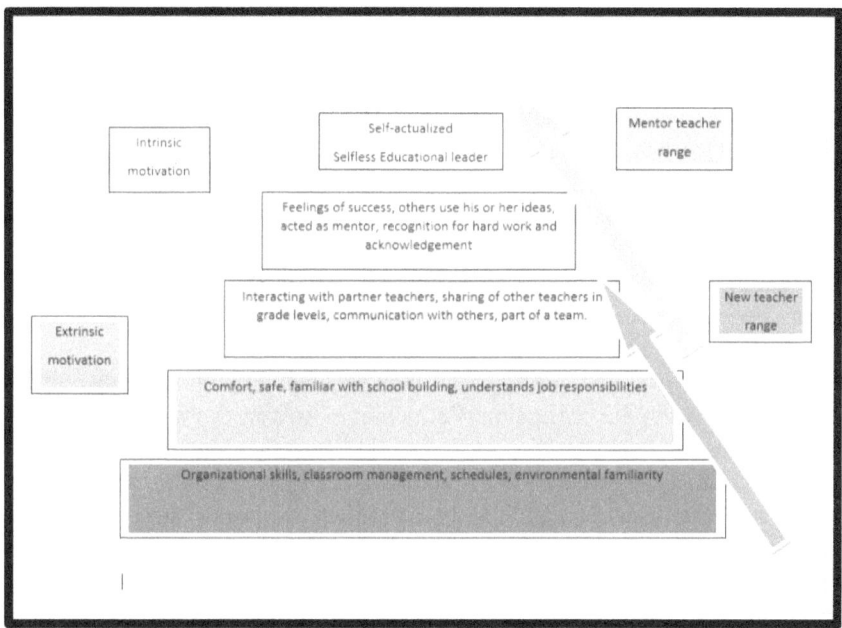

Figure 2.1. Hierarchy of Teachers' Needs Chart (Sorbet, 2018).

fits, (d) company policy and administration, (e) quality of supervision, (f) job security, (g) working conditions, (h) work and life balance, and (i) work itself (Hertzberg, 1966). These are known as extrinsic factors because they refer to the basic, external needs which are at the lower end of Maslow's Hierarchy of Needs (1943).

In considering these motivator factors, Herzberg focused on the ability to obtain personal achievement and psychological growth (Frase, 1989). It is important for managers and supervisors to be able to differentiate between motivators and hygiene factors. Hygiene factors may lead to greater levels of job satisfaction but do not necessarily add to the employees' motivation. Herzberg studied intrinsic motivational factors including achievement, recognition for achievement, responsibility, growth and advancement, and the work itself.

The interconnectedness of these theories came into education as Frase (1989) analyzed Herzberg's findings of 1966. His study attempted to differentiate between intrinsic and extrinsic motivators in the teaching profession. Intrinsic motivation is defined as being involved in an activity for its internal satisfactions rather than for some external reward. Social conditions that support feelings of competence, autonomy, and relatedness are what help to maintain intrinsic motivation (Deci, Koestner, & Ryan, 1999).

Frase found that intrinsic rewards serve as motivators, and teachers tend to get the greatest satisfaction from simply reaching and educating their students and only secondly from job recognition. Of the teachers Frase (1989) surveyed in his study, each could choose either professional travel (intrinsic motivator to enhance learning) or cash (extrinsic motivator or hygiene factor) as a motivator.

These intrinsic and extrinsic motivators are compared to those of Herzberg's Two-Factor Theory of Motivation (1966). The teachers who favored professional travel reported larger increases in professional development opportunities, which he also labeled as intrinsic motivators. His study supported the belief that school boards and administrators cannot buy teachers' motivation through salary raises.

There is a positive relationship between satisfaction with teaching and the intent to remain in the profession (Perrachione, Rosser, & Petersen, 2008). It is important to determine the intrinsic and extrinsic influences of teacher satisfaction to best assist school administrators to maintain an experienced workforce as well as to help in the search for new teachers (2008).

Mentoring provides new teachers with mentors' skills and knowledge of teaching along with their expertise and wisdom. Mentoring also provides veteran teachers with the opportunity to pass on their experiences of teaching to new teachers, which could possibly complete their careers as veteran teachers (Ganser, 1997). Mentoring is a productive and professional model that can help new teachers while providing experienced or veteran teachers a unique way to contribute to the teaching profession (Ganser, 1997). Mentoring is

> a shared role that requires delicate and caring intervention and feedback. It is a slow process built on mutual trust and self-respect. This relationship works when both mentor and protégé understand what areas need improvement. It is a teaching position carried on in a classroom setting that requires new, tactful approaches and skills. (Fibkins, 2002, p. 3)

A focused and systematic mentoring program has a positive influence on the performance of the new teacher, but it also has many advantages for the mentor teacher (Holloway, 2001). This positive and reciprocal relationship ultimately benefits the mentor and facilitates student achievement.

By comparing Maslow's Hierarchy of Needs with the Hierarchy of Teachers' Needs we can see factors that are either intrinsic or extrinsic as described in Herzberg's Two-Factory Theory of Motivation. We can also determine what factors influence new teachers beginning their careers at the lowest level of the Hierarchy of Teachers' Needs (see Figure 2.1). In Maslow's Hierarchy of Needs, the first basic level of need is food, water, warmth, and rest, while the first level of teacher needs includes the basic desire to find organizational skills, classroom management, schedules, and environmental familiarity.

As the new teachers progress throughout their professional careers, they move upward through these beginning extrinsic factors. The mentor and new teacher relationship encourages this growth upward as it allows the new teacher to become far more interested in the mentoring relationship and the collaborative process of mentoring to problem solve and set goals for students (Ganser, 1997). These interests are primarily intrinsic motivators that the mentor teacher is instilling in the new teacher.

The second level of the Hierarchy of Teachers' Needs chart, much like Maslow's second level, describes comfort and safety, and adds familiarity with school building and job responsibilities. The new teachers are steadily climbing through the extrinsic factors as they gain experience in the teaching profession.

The new teachers gain experience and slowly arrive at the stage where they are interacting with partner teachers, sharing among other teachers within their grade levels, and learning how to communicate in professional learning communities and with others as they act as part of a team. Through this climb the new teachers might possibly become mentor teachers after three years or more.

The mentor teacher range is the area of the chart where the intrinsic motivational factors begin. Here the veteran teachers serving as mentors have reached feelings of success at the level of recognition of hard work where others are asking for advice and they are being approached to mentor other teachers.

The veteran mentor teachers reach the final and highest level of the chart when they are self-actualized, described very similarly in Maslow's Hierarchy of Needs. At this level is the selfless leader who is willing to assist and support others in the profession for the personal gain of intrinsic satisfaction and contribution to the field of education.

During the mentor and mentee exchange, the mentors begin to take on challenging work as they assist and support the new teachers with challenges of the new position in the teaching profession. The new teachers experience the challenges ranked low on the teacher needs scale such as classroom management, organizational skills, scheduling, and basic environmental familiarity.

The mentors are also challenged as they assist the new teacher to raise their feelings to the second level of needs, which include comfort, safety, and general familiarity with school building and job responsibilities. The new teachers are challenged as they continue to climb through the extrinsic factors in the profession.

Motivation can span across various levels, and types of motivation may differ depending on the experience of the teacher. It is of utmost importance for school administrators to determine the intrinsic and extrinsic influences of teacher satisfaction to best maintain an experienced workforce as well as to help in the search for new teachers. Educational leaders should look at job satisfaction and motivation as key indicators in teacher retention.

There are areas of growth for both parties within a mentoring exchange. The three areas of reciprocal exchange in a mentoring relationship include (a) reflection, (b) growth, and (c) challenge. The lowest level of reciprocal exchange is challenge. During the mentor and mentee exchange, mentors begin to take on challenging work as they assist and support the mentees with the challenges of the new position in the teaching profession.

Mentees experience the challenges ranked low on the teacher needs scale such as classroom management, organizational skills, scheduling, and basic environmental familiarity. The new teachers are challenged as they continue to climb through the extrinsic factors in the profession.

The second area of reciprocity is growth. The new teachers grow professionally in this process as they lean on the mentors and mature intellectually. The mentors assist in bringing the new teachers through the basic needs of teaching to arrive higher on the Hierarchy of Teachers' Needs chart. The mentor teachers grow in task development through improving their ability to assess student learning, improve teaching strategies, and heighten their use of questioning methods (Olson, 2008).

The highest area of reciprocity within a mentoring relationship is the area of reflection. Mentoring promotes self-analysis of mentors' own teaching practices, which include teaching students and learning as their own career develops (Ganser, 1997). The mentees become more reflective practitioners as they provide feedback and assist the new teachers in areas of planning, curriculum design, organization, management, and overall instruction of students. The mentees reflect on instruction and determine what worked well and what should be adjusted.

The results of Sorbet's (2018) study indicate that mentors and mentees are motivated by differing levels of the *Areas of Reciprocity within a Mentoring Exchange*. Mentors' and mentees' motivation came primarily from the intrinsic need for a challenge within the Areas of Reciprocity within a Mentoring Exchange. Qualitative data showed that mentors saw reflection as the area in which they gained the most in the relationship, while mentees thought growth was their largest gain.

In looking at the Areas of Reciprocity within a Mentoring Exchange, Sorbet's study indicates that mentoring relationships encourage both mentors and mentees to grow stronger within their profession. If challenge, reflection, and growth were what was gained in this relationship in this order, then both mentors and mentees were driven while engaged within a mentoring relationship due to some intrinsic motivational factors.

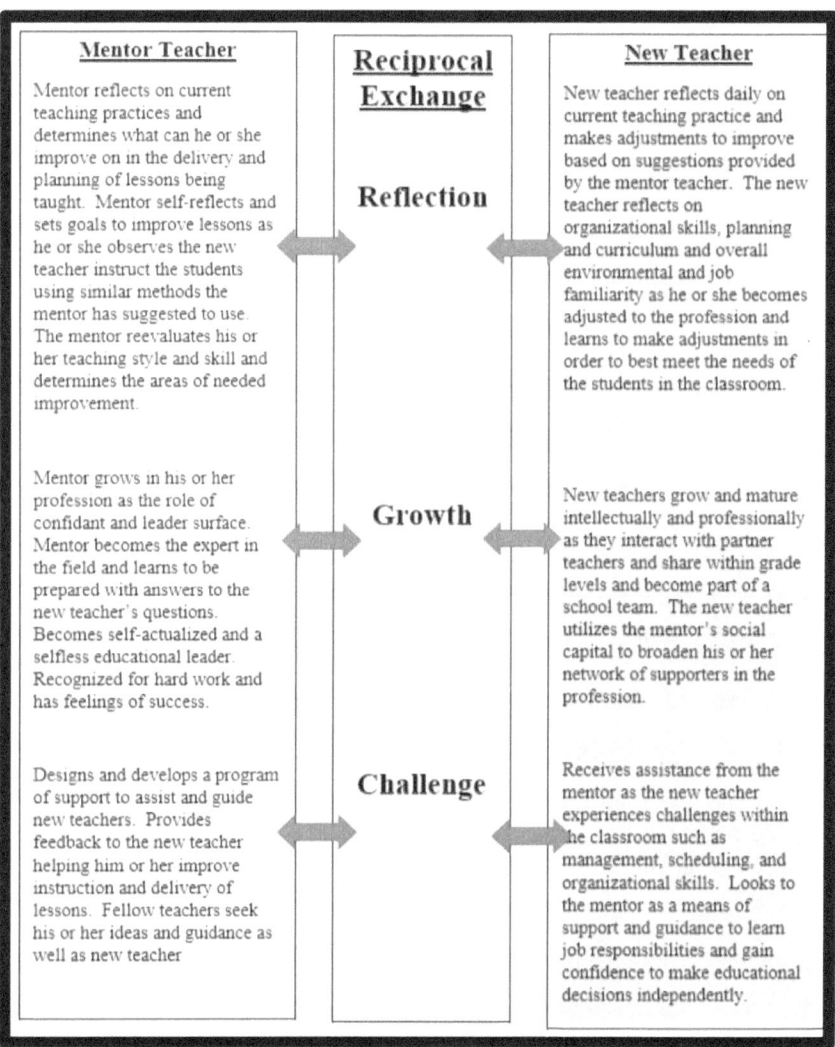

Figure 2.2. Areas of Reciprocity within a Mentoring Exchange and Emergent Themes (Sorbet, 2018).

Mentors and mentees engage in a mentoring relationship gaining (a) challenge, (b) reflection, and (c) growth. Through this reciprocal relationship, the mentor and mentee become more engaged in the profession, thus creating a stronger presence of intrinsic motivation, which is the driving force in motivating employees (Herzberg, 1959).

If motivated employees are more likely to remain in the profession, then this idea of motivation can also increase teacher retention (Perrachione, Rosser, & Petersen, 2008). There is a positive relationship between satisfaction with teaching and the intent to remain in the profession. It is important to determine the intrinsic and extrinsic influences of teacher satisfaction to best assist school administrators to maintain an experienced workforce and help in the search for new teachers (2008).

Fostering reciprocal relationships between the mentor and the mentee can be a means of motivating our teachers through instilling reflection, growth, and challenge. If a mentee and a mentor are engaged within a mentoring relationship, then reciprocal intrinsic motivation can develop from within. Intrinsically motivating mentors and mentees, specifically in areas of reflection, growth, and challenge, can improve job satisfaction. Improving job satisfaction in both new and veteran teachers can be the driving force behind new and veteran teacher retention.

KEY POINTS

Mentoring has been proven to provide benefits for both the mentor teacher and the new teacher. Through implementing mentoring programs the veteran teacher grows as he or she increases self-awareness and reflective practices in teaching techniques while supporting and assisting the new teacher to grow in the profession. This relationship encourages bonds and lasting friendships that instill intrinsic motivation from within, thus encouraging teachers to remain in the profession. This chapter provides research to support the need for mentoring programs to be established within schools to support teachers both veteran and new.

Chapter Three

Roles

Team of Leaders

This book is designed for use by school-level administrators, principals, beginning teachers, mentors, and coaches within the kindergarten through twelfth grades. By following the recommendations presented in this guide, coaches, administrators, and mentors should create a type of learning community centered around the beginning teacher using processes and tools as a reference and a plan to provide ongoing support for the beginning teacher in his or her first year of teaching.

Several roles are described in these sections. It is recognized that all schools may not have the personnel in place to fulfill all the roles specified. The ideas presented on the next several pages represent recommended practices, and it is realized that each school will approach establishing a mentor program through a different lens or point of view.

As a guide, there may be some recommendations that have not been previously considered. As with anything, thoughtful attention and conversation with other stakeholders will likely yield a program that fits the unique character of each school. Having said that, perhaps the most important functions are the ones served by a collaborative team.

COLLABORATION TEAM'S ROLES

Before engaging in any specific tasks associated with the work of establishing a mentoring program, a professional learning community or collaboration team should be established between the administration, mentor, and coach.

According to Hall and Hord (2006), a professional learning community is a "network of conversations" (p. 32).

This sort of learning community provides a space and time to come together as a team and discuss common areas of concern. Through mentoring, the professional learning community comes together to discover methods of assisting the beginning teacher based on newly identified data and techniques in the field of study. It is recommended that the team use collaborative teaming processes such as frequent face-to-face interactions that incorporate mutual accountability and shared leadership.

This community or collaboration team works in unison to create a culture of beliefs as to which type of support and professional development is needed based on the performance of the beginning teacher throughout the first three years of instruction. The learning community meets regularly to develop and establish expectations of the varying roles in the tasks of mentoring, coaching, and supporting beginning teachers.

It is imperative that the collaborative team approach all their work from a positive and proactive point of view. Efforts must focus on assisting the new teacher and nurturing him or her, providing support in a safe and supportive environment. Conversations that target the developing teacher must incorporate the beginning teacher's voice, and all discussions which address growth are to remain confidential. Nothing discourages trust as much as a conversation that finds its way into the general population.

During the collaboration meetings, the team discusses how to assist and continue to monitor the beginning teachers as they enter their second year of teaching. The team creates a timeline of visits and observations as the teachers move into their second and third years of teaching and determine the needs these teachers may have. They provide time to discuss and plan ongoing professional development for the second- and third-year teachers as they are retained but continue to require support in the profession.

Individual collaboration teams meet regularly to discuss the needs of their new teachers. Collectively, all collaboration teams on the school's campus occasionally come together to discuss the general needs of all of the mentees to aid in the creation of necessary professional development.

Small- and large-group discussions take place to set forth and establish the goals of the individual school's mentoring program for the school year. Ideas are generated by faculty while they work through the logistics of implementing the program to assist and retain beginning teachers.

The collaboration team meets to discuss initial progress and areas of weakness and strengths. Together the collaboration team has a set day, time, and location to work on a plan together to address the mentee's areas of targeted improvement throughout the school year. The collaborative team is responsible for incorporating the mentee's professional growth goals and self-identified areas of struggle throughout the mentoring process.

The collaboration team meets after subsequent new teacher evaluations, and the new teacher's progress is again measured. Evidence of growth and struggle is provided by the new teacher as well as others who have worked closely with the mentee. At this time goals are revisited, adjusted, changed, or reaffirmed. Ongoing support is provided as the new teacher grows, accomplishes milestones, and moves forward through the first year.

Share fairs, or a time to share ideas and thoughts, might be set up with other collaboration teams at the school site as well as possibly located at other participating school sites within the district. Share fairs provide a time for the faculty to bring ideas about professional development, classroom organization, time management, and basic logistics as to how they implemented the change to one place where they can share these ideas with other schools.

These share fairs are held throughout the school year to headline what worked best and what was needed in the implementation of the change so that faculty involved can gain new information from each other as to what helped to support their beginning teachers. The information gained from conversations with the other area schools that have already implemented the mentoring program is presented in a discussion with the members of the collaboration team.

A share fair gives the new teacher and the team an opportunity to celebrate progress and ideas with others who are participating in the new mentoring program. Videos of actual implementation of aspects of the mentoring program such as coaching in a classroom, beginning teachers' retreat, mentoring discussions, and providing appropriate feedback are available to new schools adopting the process.

It is during the times when the team meets that areas of needed improvement are highlighted and the remediation or assistance process begins. The areas on the teacher evaluation that need improvement are targeted with professional development, observations of fellow and mentor teachers at the school site, and visits to other school sites for additional observations.

PRINCIPAL'S AND ADMINISTRATOR'S ROLES

To begin implementation of this mentoring program, the administration recognizes the steps of the change process in order to guide the faculty through adoption of the mentoring program. Before explaining the steps or a timeline of the change, the administration must first explain the logic behind the change.

In order to implement the change, it is highly recommended that administrators read this guide in its entirety, decide what processes are to be implemented, and then bring forth recommendations to the faculty for discussion.

Some administrators may engage in a short book study with key stakeholders before moving forward. The administration should then discuss with the faculty why implementation is so important.

Interviews and roundtable discussions between administrators and beginning teachers in their first five years in the profession give insight into what new teachers might need during their first year of teaching. Information such as this is presented to the faculty involved in a manner that allows the organization to understand the necessity of the implementation.

The administration first presents the research information and ideas that back the need for this change to the faculty involved. Teacher retention is very important and a major contributor to the student success rate. The administration explains that in order to increase the teacher retention rate and encourage beginning teachers to stay in the profession, there are several requirements that should be put into place.

The fact that beginning teachers who are supported tend to stay longer in the field is a key understanding for all participants. If these teachers are retained, the faculty can continue to grow into a long-term faculty, creating a sense of community between all of the faculty members and allowing more learning and support of each other. To show the necessity for the program, the administration discusses the turnover rate and also shows data and results from the schools that support their teachers utilizing such a program.

Using a proactive approach, administrators provide a scope of the change that enables the faculty to understand the expectations prior to implementation. The faculty becomes fully aware of all requirements as well as changes that will occur in the upcoming months of the program. The tables in this chapter outline the expectations and the involvement of the mentor, coach, administrator, and peer buddy throughout the first year of support for the beginning teacher. When this mentoring program is explained and implemented, the faculty involved are provided a copy of the expectations and are invited to choose the dates to target these observations.

The administration conducts the initial evaluation while observing the beginning teacher within the first quarter of the school year and provides results in a timely manner. Beginning teachers conference with the administration about areas of improvement and growth.

A copy of the evaluation is provided to the collaboration team, and the team discusses and cocreates with the novice teacher the semester developmental goals to work on targeted areas that were observed during the initial lesson. The administration observes the beginning teacher again at the start of the third quarter of school and notes if the teacher is making progress on his or her developmental goals and areas of focus for improvement. The principal is a valuable part of the professional learning community or collaboration team who assists the teacher in that first year.

Administrators may initially be concerned about who they will select to become mentor teachers, peer buddies, and coaches to assist the beginning teacher. The administration may also question which faculty members will have the ability to become a mentor or peer buddy or if they will be identified to serve in such a role.

During the training phase, the administration provides the faculty involved with the requirements of their roles as well as the requirements for the beginning teachers. Release time is also provided for the new teacher while he or she observes another veteran teacher who can model appropriate instructional strategies in their subject or grade level.

An Administrator's Checklist to Help the Beginning Teacher in the Classroom

- Observe
- Set goals for implementation
- Monitor teacher and collaboration team
- Check on beginning teacher often
- Offer support and discussion
- Provide resources with information
- Provide release time for professional development
- Assign mentor
- Assign peer buddy
- Meet regularly with coach
- Provide positive comments with supportive and reassuring feedback

MENTOR'S ROLES

The beginning teacher or mentee receives a mentor. A mentor is referred to by Rowley (1999) as someone who is committed to assisting them to be successful in the profession. The mentor attends a workshop offered by the

Table 3.1. Number of observations of beginning teachers by administration

	First-year teacher	Second-year teacher	Third-year teacher
Mentor visits	Weekly	Monthly	Once per semester
Coach visits	Monthly	Bimonthly	Once per semester
Administration observations	Quarterly	Once per semester	Once per semester
Peer buddy collaboration	Daily	Daily to weekly	Weekly

administration or school district to train him or her on the proper ways to mentor a beginning teacher. During training, the mentor learns how to provide appropriate and encouraging feedback to the beginning teacher in order to properly mentor the teacher in becoming successful in the profession.

Committed mentors hold high standards and expect both themselves and mentees to rise to the challenge of the job. Mentors work extremely closely with the novice teachers, and it is imperative that the relationship is one of trust, mutual accountability, and respect. Once again, confidentiality is critical when discussing areas of growth and struggle.

During the mentee's first year, the mentor provides demonstrations of quality lessons for the beginning teacher to observe as well as evaluate and provides feedback on observed lessons of the mentee throughout the first year of teaching. A mentor is assigned to the mentee who will demonstrate methods of instruction.

The mentor is located on campus near the mentee so she or he can provide ongoing assistance and modeling for instructional practices throughout the first three years. The mentor is available to provide ongoing assistance with the day-to-day routines and challenges that the beginning teacher would encounter in the classroom at the school site.

Mentors are able to see the change and results in other schools that have implemented a mentoring program. They see the mentees gain confidence and advance in the profession as the first year progresses onward. Open discussions and conversations throughout the introduction of the program will motivate the mentor to visualize a hands-on approach to assisting and supporting beginning teachers.

Mentors will express concern to administrators about time restraints for training and for implementing the change. These teachers will express concern about managing their classrooms as well as having to support and provide feedback to a beginning teacher. During initial mentoring training, the mentor may need information and organizational ideas to be able to time manage and multitask well in order to feel confident in becoming a successful mentor teacher.

Mentors are allowed to observe other mentor teachers in the district and collaborate with them on best practices for mentoring beginning teachers. Mentor teachers are provided with release time (consider parent volunteer support or duty-free days) that will allow mentoring and collaboration to take place. Along with release time, continuing learning units are also awarded to mentors for this type of assistance throughout the school year.

The mentor assigned to the new teacher receives a copy of the initial review to be able to properly assist the beginning teacher throughout the school year. During the second quarter of the school year, the mentor observes the beginning teacher to check for improvements prior to the administrator's second observation. The mentor and the beginning teacher are given release time from the classroom through the use of parent volunteers to provide observable lessons for the beginning teacher that target those areas that are in need of improvement.

A Mentor's Checklist to Help the Beginning Teacher in the Classroom

- Observe
- Set goals
- Set up time to assist while beginning teacher goes to observe
- Provide quality lessons for observation
- Journal with beginning teacher
- Model appropriate professionalism
- Demonstrate appropriate contact with parents
- Listen and be supportive
- Provide encouragement
- Provide feedback and other ideas and methods of instruction
- Provide resources

COACH'S ROLES

Coaching is a confidential process and involves two or more professionals working together in a myriad of ways, including reflection on practice, refining or building new skills, sharing ideas, and researching classroom practices, and solving problems (Robbins, 1991). The curriculum coach's role in the induction of the new teacher is to simply do this. The coach might be a faculty member within a teacher education program at a local college or university, a retired teacher who is still involved in the school system, or

Table 3.2. Number of observations of beginning teachers by mentor

	First-year teacher	*Second-year teacher*	*Third-year teacher*
Mentor visits	Weekly	Monthly	Once per semester
Coach visits	Monthly	Bimonthly	Once per semester
Administration observations	Quarterly	Once per semester	Once per semester
Peer buddy collaboration	Daily	Daily to weekly	Weekly

Years four and five requirements are to be determined by the collaboration team.

another veteran teacher who is in a position to assist throughout the district or within the school.

The curriculum coach acts as a helping teacher in the classroom and is assigned to a group of four to five beginning teachers. Spending time with the beginning teacher during and after school while counseling and coaching helps his or her teachers become better able to grow professionally and become intrinsically motivated through the first year. As a confidant, the coach provides moral support, materials, and other classroom management assistance to the beginning teacher as needed.

The assigned coach visits the beginning teacher monthly; provides a day of assistance with instruction, paperwork, curriculum alignment, and resources; and simply acts as a confidant to the beginning teacher. Providing a place and time where all of the beginning teachers within his or her group could go to collaborate and talk about the ongoing challenges they are facing is an important part of the coach's function. The coach also utilizes the suggested processes to keep track of the areas the beginning teacher needs.

The coach also provides training for the mentors in the early stages of the implementation process. The coach uses the most current statewide teacher evaluation tools to bring attention to the beginning teacher's strategies of effective teaching in the classroom. The coach works in conjunction with the administration and mentor to assist the new teacher in working through various topics throughout the school year.

A Coach's Checklist to Help the Beginning Teacher in the Classroom

- Provide support and counsel
- Set up regular visits
- Provide curriculum resources
- Provide ideas for professional development and furthering education
- Model appropriate professionalism
- Listen and be supportive
- Provide encouragement
- Provide feedback
- Assist with paperwork, centers, instruction, and other daily duties the teacher needs

PEER BUDDY'S ROLES

Peer buddies are also established within the collaboration teams. A peer buddy teacher who teaches the same grade level or subject area can be assigned to a beginning teacher to provide additional feedback and resources

Table 3.3. Number of observations of beginning teachers by coach

	First-year teacher	Second-year teacher	Third-year teacher
Mentor visits	Weekly	Monthly	Once per semester
Coach visits	Monthly	Bimonthly	Once per semester
Administration observations	Quarterly	Once per semester	Once per semester
Peer buddy collaboration	Daily	Daily to weekly	Weekly

Year four and five requirements are to be determined by the collaboration team.

throughout the school year. Peer buddies express concerns about the level of assistance they will be required to provide. Peer buddies share lesson ideas and materials, listen to ideas from the beginning teacher, provide information for upcoming due dates and requirements, and also assist the beginning teacher in any daily tasks.

A Peer Buddy's Checklist to Help the Beginning Teacher in the Classroom

- Provide quality lessons for observation
- Model appropriate professionalism
- Demonstrate appropriate contact with parents
- Listen and be supportive
- Provide encouragement
- Provide feedback and other ideas and methods of instruction
- Provide resources
- Show examples of lessons
- Share lesson plans and resources

BEGINNING TEACHER'S ROLES

Teachers within their first five years of teaching are invited to provide insight as to which areas they needed assistance with when they were in the first three years of teaching. Beginning teachers evaluate and discuss the needs that they encountered during their first year teaching during roundtable discussions.

When beginning teachers are introduced to the general information about the district and school in which they are teaching, they will likely become aware of the expectations at the district and school level as far as student

Table 3.4. Number of observations of beginning teachers by peer buddy

	First-year teacher	Second-year teacher	Third-year teacher
Mentor visits	Weekly	Monthly	Once per semester
Coach visits	Monthly	Bimonthly	Once per semester
Administration observations	Quarterly	Once per semester	Once per semester
Peer buddy collaboration	Daily	Daily to weekly	Weekly

Year four and five requirements are to be determined by the collaboration team.

achievement, teacher evaluation and expectations, and parental communication. Beginning teachers receive a timeline of events at the beginning of the school year to outline the annual expectations and requirements for the entire school year well in advance. Table 3.5 details the observations that the beginning teacher might encounter throughout the first year of teaching. The beginning teacher is presented with this chart at the start of the school year and is allowed to work with the other members of the collaboration team to decide the best dates for their observations. This ongoing collaboration with the team helps new teachers feel both supported and cared for as they navigate through their first years as novices.

A Beginning Teacher's Checklist to Being a First-Year Teacher

- Observe mentor teachers
- Set goals
- Meet with collaboration team
- Journal with mentor
- Converse with peer buddy daily
- Listen and ask good questions
- Accept feedback and constructive criticism and be easily coachable and approachable
- Follow school and district rules and policies
- Be an example for students

Table 3.5. Observation requirements for beginning teachers in years one to three

	First-year teacher	Second-year teacher	Third-year teacher
Observe mentor teacher	Monthly	Quarterly	Once a semester
Observe peer buddy teacher	Weekly to monthly	Once a semester	As needed
Observe off-site teacher	Once a semester	As needed	As needed

Year four and five requirements are to be determined by the collaboration team.

Table 3.6. Collaboration requirements for beginning teachers in years one to three

	First-year teacher	Second-year teacher	Third-year teacher
Collaborate with peer buddy	Daily	Daily	Daily
Collaborate with mentor teacher	Twice a week or more	Weekly	Monthly
Collaborate with coaches	Weekly	Monthly	Once per semester
Collaborate with administration	Weekly	Weekly	Weekly

Year four and five requirements will be determined by the collaboration team.

KEY POINTS

This chapter identifies the specific roles for the collaboration team, principal or administrator, mentor, coach, peer buddy, and new teacher involved in a mentoring program. Included is a detailed description of the roles as well as the expectations of duties such as collaborations and observations. This chapter also addresses some basic concerns members of the collaboration team may have.

As schools adopt a mentoring program for new teachers, it is imperative that roles be clearly defined and that timelines be established. The success of new teachers depends on surrounding them with a well-developed and highly committed team. Collaboration teams work best when they meet regularly, work toward the same goal, and share responsibilities for assisting the new teacher. In addition, the collaboration team honors the voice of the novice teacher by incorporating his or her goals for improvement into the discussion.

Chapter Four

Navigating through Change

Undertaking a new approach to mentorship generally requires professional development for all stakeholders in processes to be adopted and roles to be assumed. While embarking on this journey, administrators are heavily invested in the training of mentors, coaches, and peer buddies, all with the goal of assisting the beginning teacher in the first three years of teaching.

This guide is designed to be used at the independent school building level for beginning teachers within their first three years of teaching in kindergarten through twelfth grade. Providing a firm foundation takes a deep examination of numerous factors. In this chapter, the change process will be further explored, and the Concerns-Based Adoption Model (CBAM) will be discussed in detail. Administrators should take into careful consideration the climate and culture of their school and present the information regarding the new mentorship program in manageable stages to maximize effectiveness.

There is a common misconception among administrators and leaders today. Many educational leaders believe that once an innovation is introduced and members of the organization are provided professional development, the change is then put into action. However, positive change occurs over time, and organizational members experience a variety of needs as they go through the change.

As with any innovation, implementing a mentoring program successfully takes considerable time and understanding to be able to address the individual concerns that each novice and veteran teacher brings to the process. It is only through a deep appreciation of each educator's perspectives that an attentive educational leader can fully address individual concerns.

This guide leads the K–12 teacher, mentor, coach, peer buddy, or other faculty involved through the change process utilizing CBAM (Hall & Hord,

2006). CBAM has helped educational leaders by addressing each stage of concern of all individuals involved in the change.

In this chapter, CBAM will be discussed, and the components of the model will be reviewed. Although the entire model is not used in the new mentoring program, it is helpful to see those pieces recommended for use within a larger context.

Frequently, when educators are faced with the task of implementing a new intervention, they come to the process of change. The process of change is a developmental process and individuals will vary in the stages they are in. Some will go through the process faster than others. Individuals can also be in multiple stages at once. There are some who are familiar with the program under consideration, some who have never heard of the program, and some who have varying degrees of experience with the program.

For those who work with teachers, facilitating and leading the process of program implementation can be met with excitement, frustration, or even anger at the suggestion of something new or different being tried (Knight, 2007). It is critical that those who provide leadership during the change are keenly aware of how those responsible at the classroom level (the teachers) are receiving the change. This can be daunting for everyone concerned.

The Stages of Concern Questionnaire (SOCQ) from the CBAM framework has been used for measuring implementation of practices and facilitating change. Using the SOCQ to help professional developers understand how teachers fall on a continuum of concern is one way to facilitate implementation of a new program.

In addition to assisting educators in understanding the myriad elements of the change process, SOCQ can be used to ensure that professional development activities and processes will help increase the likelihood that student success will be positively impacted. For those who engage in planning and supporting change with classroom teachers, it is imperative that an understanding of participants, including their concerns and their level of readiness, is folded into the process of change.

SOCQ provides a means of understanding where teachers fall on a continuum that spans from the awareness stage (gaining interest in the intervention) through the refocusing stage (concentrating on new developments and interests beyond the current intervention). CBAM collectively provides a framework for measuring the application and utilization of change-inducing tools or procedures in order to facilitate lasting effective development. Through this model, educators can grow in their understanding of how they respond to the process of change and the change itself.

By gaining an understanding of both the change and the process of change, CBAM ensures that potential actions can be taken to facilitate successful change, and professional development activities with the greatest potential impact can be provided to those who are being affected by new programs. Using the framework provided by CBAM increases the chances that the person(s) undergoing change will be positively impacted by professional development and systematic change (Saunders, 2012).

According to George, Hall, and Stiegelbauer (2006), "the CBAM research team believed that change begins with the individual, usually the teacher or adopter, and focused its early efforts on understanding what happens to teachers and college faculty when presented with a change" (p. 1). CBAM consists of three diagnostic dimensions: the Innovation Configuration, the Levels of Use, and the Stages of Concern.

Educators often spend a considerable amount of time learning new or evolving school programs and practices, but they are lacking when it comes to the practical application. Educators are often taught what a program is. They are not taught what it looks like when it is carried out in real time.

The diagnostic area of Innovation Configuration addresses this by providing expectations, descriptions, and guides for each individual person involved in the program. By using this tool, every educator that the program affects is able to see a clear depiction of what the program looks like from their particular stance. With this comes Innovation Configuration maps that chart out the distinct ways a person may go about implementing the program or practice in a functional, pragmatic way.

Levels of Use is another section of CBAM that is useful at the individual change level. The Levels of Use consists of an interview tool that informs educators how both themselves and others are realistically using a program. To accomplish this, the diagnostic tool encompasses eight levels that depict where an educator is in implementing a change by their current actions in the program. Multiple brief interviews are conducted to confer an individual's ongoing level of use. The levels are as follows: nonuse, orientation, preparation, mechanical use, routine use, refinement, integration, and renewal.

The CBAM tool used in the new teacher mentoring program is pulled from the third category: Stages of Concern. SOCQ was initially used for the purpose of evaluating teachers, and was developed in the 1970s by Hall and Loucks. SOCQ was designed to look primarily at trainee concerns and the affective experience of change. The Stages of Concern as a full unit includes a questionnaire, interview, and open-ended statements to measure an individual educator's beliefs and position regarding the implementation of change.

As described by Bailey and Palsha (1992), the Stages of Concern assumes that change is an ongoing, personal development that is mediated by training and can be matched to the expressed concerns of the individuals. The Stages of Concern consists of seven distinct categories: awareness, informational, personal, management, consequence, collaborative, and refocusing.

The seven categories from the Stages of Concern are defined here. First is *awareness* (not concerned with change and not interested in implementation), then *informational* (beginning to show interest and would like to know

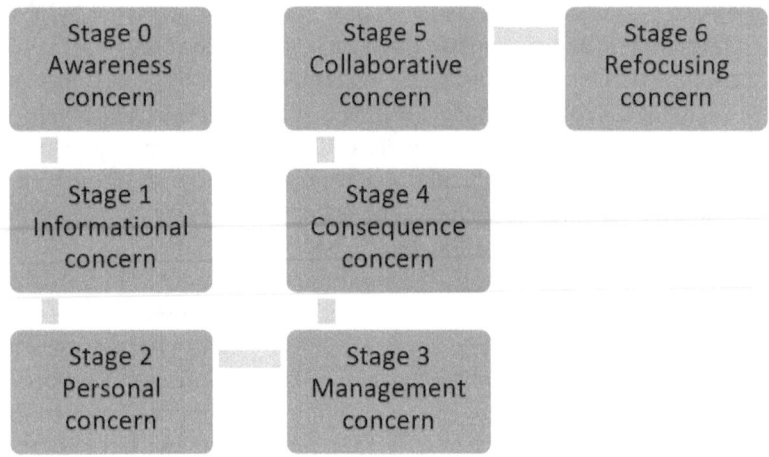

Figure 4.1. Stages of Concern Flowchart.

more about the intervention/innovation), followed by *personal* (beginning to think about how a change might directly affect them). Next comes *management* (beginning preparation, thinking about resources and application), *consequence* (concerned how change will impact students), *collaborative* (interested in sharing innovation with others), and, finally, *refocusing* (exploring ideas for making the innovation better or how it might be improved upon).

Thus, questions arise such as "Is the educator ready to make a change? What are the educator's personal thoughts on the program or practice? Is the educator uncomfortable with the change process altogether?" These types of questions and feelings are worked through to identify where the educator stands. The overarching theoretical idea is that the farther along in the seven Stages of Concern categories an educator is, the more likely an effective change will occur.

SOCQ is a 35-item questionnaire that functions to categorize and assess concerns surrounding potential change in programs and practices. The individual taking the questionnaire will fall into one of the seven categories above (awareness, informational, personal, management, consequence, collaborative, refocusing) by being scored on their responses to the questions found in SOCQ.

If an individual falls into a category such as collaborative or refocusing, they are likely to have less concern about the implementation of the new program or practice. On the other end of the spectrum, scores that fit into the informational or personal categories would indicate more concern from the individual regarding the change.

Change and reform are associated with raising teacher quality and improving student learning, achievement, and preparedness. Thus, it is important that teachers receive the systematic and sustained support to move out of their comfort zones and implement a program or practice (Christesen & Turner, 2014). Using SOCQ helps to identify where the individual stands regarding the change, and proper actions can be determined to facilitate action.

Utilizing a model such as CBAM when implementing change within an organization allows individual organizational members' needs to be acknowledged throughout the change process (Hall & Hord, 2006). CBAM applies attention to the concerns of the individuals involved in or experiencing the change. CBAM allows administrators and leaders to look at the implemented change through the multiple perspectives of all involved while carrying out the change.

There is great need for educational leaders to utilize such an approach when implementing change. Leaders within an organization must recognize there may be resistance to any change that will be brought to an organization. When rolling out such a change as creating a mentoring program and establishing mentoring partnerships between new and veteran teachers, everyone's concerns are considered. These concerns are addressed prior to the dissemination of the information outlined within this guide and the implementation of the program.

Concerns of beginning teachers who enter the first year of the profession include feeling bogged down with organizing their classrooms and preparing for their first day of class. With these pressing issues, attending a retreat or another induction meeting may seem to be too time-consuming. Any task that is not directly tied to being in the classroom in preparation for the new year may seem to be too daunting.

New teachers may show resistance toward going through teacher retreats and/or professional development due to the fact that they feel initially overwhelmed. These new teachers may want to focus on getting their classrooms ready and plan for the students they will be receiving and may not be as attentive in new teacher meetings or retreats as one would expect. These concerns are real to the new teacher and are heard and validated throughout the change process.

Veteran teachers have different concerns than those of new teachers. Veteran teachers may feel overwhelmed with time constraints of their own and may not want to take on a mentee. Veteran teachers may show resentment toward a new mentoring program in that they did not have such a supportive network when they were beginning teachers.

Veteran teachers may feel so overwhelmed with their own schedules that taking on a new teacher to mentor may cause additional anxiety or stress. The administration recognizes and addresses these concerns and reassures the faculty members that the change being implemented will not only assist beginning teachers but will also provide an opportunity for veteran teachers to grow and move into new and engaging leadership roles.

The targeted areas addressed by CBAM, such as curriculum, classroom management, and role as a professional, were chosen to provide more detail in each of three general areas of concern for all involved. The mentor, beginning teacher, coach, and peer buddy are to address these main areas of concern as research shows that these are the most crucial areas of need for the new teacher. Other areas of concern may arise and should be carefully addressed throughout the implementation process.

A timeline has been put into place to lay out all of the requirements for the mentor, administrator, coach, and peer buddy as well as the beginning teacher for the first three years of teaching. The timelines are located in chapter 12. This book outlines the roles of all involved within this change and the best ways that they are to support and model best practices for the beginning teacher.

KEY POINTS

This chapter provides general information that supports the need to address individual concerns within an organization that is experiencing change. CBAM is defined here and the need for using such a model to implement change is described. Although the entire model is not utilized in the new teacher mentoring program, an understanding of where participants fall on a continuum of change adoption is critical for planning appropriate interventions and assistance.

Chapter Five

Addressing Concerns for Beginning Teachers

To address areas of concern for the beginning teacher when implementing a mentoring program, it is suggested that Hall and Hord's Stages of Concern (2006) be utilized. The Southwest Educational Development Laboratory, or SEDL, has taken this model and adapted it for teachers.

SEDL has worked to improve teaching and learning through research and technical assistance for over 50 years. The mission is "to strengthen the connections among research, policy, and practice in order to improve outcomes for all learners" (http://www.sedl.org/about/).

The various concerns teachers may exhibit are later addressed in this section of the guide. Accompanying each possible concern, there are basic explanations of ways to address them in the varying phases of the developmental process of the plan. Below are the stages of concern for the beginning teacher in the order in which they are to be presented.

Stage 0—Awareness Concerns

- If possible, involve teachers in discussions and decisions about the innovation and its implementation.
- Share enough information to arouse interest, but not so much that it overwhelms.
- Acknowledge that a lack of awareness is expected and reasonable, and that no questions about the innovation are foolish.
- Encourage unaware persons to talk with colleagues who know about the innovation.
- Take steps to minimize gossip and inaccurate sharing of information about the innovation.

Stage 1—Informational Concerns

- Provide clear and accurate information about the innovation.
- Use a variety of ways to share information—verbally, in writing, and through any available media. Communicate with individuals and with small and large groups.
- Have persons who have used the innovation in other settings visit with your teachers. Visits to other schools can also be arranged.
- Help teachers see how the innovation relates to their current practices, both in regard to similarities and differences.
- Be enthusiastic and enhance the visibility of others who are excited.

Stage 2—Personal Concerns

- Legitimize the existence and expression of personal concerns. Knowing these concerns are common and that others have them can be comforting.
- Use personal notes and conversations to provide encouragement and reinforce personal adequacy.
- Connect these teachers with others whose personal concerns have diminished and who will be supportive.
- Show how the innovation can be implemented sequentially rather than in one big leap. It is important to establish expectations that are attainable.
- Do not push innovation use, but encourage and support it while maintaining expectations.

Stage 3—Management Concerns

- Clarify the steps and components of the innovation. Information from innovation configurations will be helpful here.
- Provide answers that address the small specific "how-to" issues that are so often the cause of management concerns.
- Demonstrate exact and practical solutions to the logistical problems that contribute to the concerns.
- Help teachers sequence specific activities and set timelines for their accomplishments.
- Attend to the immediate demands of the innovation, not what will be or can be in the future.

Stage 4—Consequence Concerns

- Provide these individuals with opportunities to visit other settings where the innovation is in use and to attend conferences on the topic.
- Don't overlook these individuals. Give them positive feedback and needed support.
- Find opportunities for these persons to share their skills with others.
- Share information pertaining to the innovation.

Stage 5—Collaborative Concerns

- Provide these individuals with opportunities to develop those skills necessary for working collaboratively.
- Bring together those persons, both within and outside the school, who are interested in collaboration.
- Help the collaborators establish reasonable expectations and timelines for the collaborative effort.
- Use these persons to provide technical assistance to others who need assistance.
- Encourage the collaborators, but don't attempt to force collaboration on those who are not interested.

Stage 6—Refocusing Concerns

- Respect and encourage the interest these persons have for finding a better way.
- Help these individuals channel their ideas and energies in ways that will be productive rather than counterproductive.
- Encourage these individuals to act on their ideas for program improvement.
- Help these persons access resources they may need to refine their ideas and put them into practice.
- Be aware of and willing to accept the fact that these persons may replace previous practices.

CONCERN OF KNOWLEDGE OF CURRICULUM AND SUBJECT MATTER

Awareness Concerns

Beginning teachers express general concern upon receiving their new teaching assignment and have their own knowledge of the subject matter to be taught. To build awareness, beginning teachers need to be given access to resources and trainers who can provide the curriculum and information for them to learn in order to instruct their students.

When beginning teachers are given access to the state standards as well as teaching basals or curriculum guides (either online access or hard copies), they are better set to be successful. Anticipating other needs, the provision of handbooks and access to relevant documents helps the new teacher feel more adequately prepared to teach.

Beginning teachers are more successful when engaged in meaningful conversations with peer buddies who are teaching within their same subject or grade level about the timeline of the curriculum for the school year. Long-range plans and any other materials that are needed are readily accessible for the beginning teacher.

Beginning teachers may be overwhelmed with the new information and are well served when they are provided with time and resources to become knowledgeable of the curriculum and information they will be responsible for. Support from peer buddies is established during this time, and beginning teachers are able to identify those veteran teachers who are capable and willing to assist in the subject matter.

Informational Concerns

To address these concerns, group discussions about the curriculum among the beginning teachers within their grade or subject level are initiated. To strengthen a response to informational concerns, technological resources are provided as well as other content knowledge material. The information is presented to the beginning teacher in an enthusiastic manner and is not intended to overwhelm the novice.

Beginning teachers begin to collect ideas when they visit teachers' classrooms at their school site and other schools. With these visits and observations of other veteran teachers who teach within the same content area, the new teacher is able to ask questions, borrow materials, and understand how the curriculum and content are presented in various ways.

New teachers will generally come with the relevant certification required to fulfill the requirements of their grade levels or subjects. Information may be needed regarding pacing guides and grade-level teams or common understandings regarding content and its delivery. It is critical that this information be provided to the new teacher at the beginning of the academic term.

Personal Concerns

Beginning teachers express personal concern of the unknown. These teachers need to feel validated for their concerns and be able to communicate their needs and wants directly. The administration and collaboration team address personal concerns by showing that they are available to assist the beginning teacher with his or her needs throughout the day and school year.

The peer buddies collaborate with the beginning teacher on ideas that may have worked in their classrooms while helping the beginning teacher learn the content and curriculum for instruction. Peers also work with the beginning teacher to plan his or her lessons. The beginning teacher is provided with a risk-free environment to ask for assistance and support from other faculty members.

Although the novice teacher comes with requisite credentials for the current classroom setting, he or she needs support in delivering instruction to a group of students he or she has never been responsible for. Encouragement takes many forms, and a supportive team uses emails, personal notes, and positive comments to help the new teacher ease into the year.

Management Concerns

The first step in assisting the beginning teacher with the curriculum and content knowledge of his or her field is to provide access to all of the materials needed for the teacher to plan quality lessons. Management concerns can be time- and energy-consuming. To assist, a laptop or computer as well as hard copies and online versions of books and teacher resources are provided for research and instruction. The beginning teacher becomes knowledgeable of deadlines for submitting lesson plans and is provided with a template containing the required components of the school's or district's lesson plans.

Sharing tricks such as file organization, collecting student work, grading student assignments, and all the management tasks associated with monitoring progress will help the new teacher with the potentially overwhelming tasks of organizing and managing a classroom full of active students. Mentors and peer buddies can all pitch in to suggest ideas that will help the fledgling teacher get a handle on all the curriculum tasks.

Consequence Concerns

With consequence concerns, beginning teachers are given release time to observe other classrooms within their subject or grade level to gain ideas and information about different approaches in instruction. These beginning teachers are allowed time to share their new ideas with other grade levels or departments within the school or district.

After a few months in the classroom, new teachers are generally feeling the ebb and flow of classroom life and have developed understanding of their students through daily contact and instruction. At this point, additional support regarding the evaluation of student outcomes and changes needed to improve student outcomes are needed. Beginning teachers are provided positive feedback and encouragement throughout their endeavors to build community and feelings of support.

Collaborative Concerns

Beginning teachers are given opportunities to attend training and professional development within their grade level or content area to target collaborative concerns. These trainings provide a better understanding of the grade or curriculum in which the novice is teaching. District personnel such as curriculum coaches and other experts are brought in to provide ongoing support and resources that are currently related to their area of expertise for the beginning teacher to utilize in his or her lesson instruction.

Beginning teachers are invited but not required to collaborate with these coaches on a regular basis to reinforce what they are implementing in their classrooms. Relationships are cultivated between the collaboration team and the new teacher in an effort to build community and rapport in the professional workspace. Coordinating and cooperating with other professionals gives the new teachers an opportunity to develop as content expert team members.

Refocusing Concerns

Some beginning teachers come to the job with the idea that they may already know where the best information is and how to best instruct the students in their classroom. To address refocusing concerns, the administration respects these individual ideas and supports the novice's methods of instruction while also providing ongoing support and innovative methods of instruction that are readily available.

The administration and collaboration team encourage beginning teachers to express their concerns about the content knowledge in discussions within teams and with peer buddies. Beginning teachers are given ample opportunities for sharing their own knowledge of the content and how to best plan and implement their own lessons while aligning them with the administration's and district's guidelines.

CONCERN OF CLASSROOM MANAGEMENT

Awareness Concerns

Beginning teachers have concerns regarding the basic managing and arranging of the classroom. To address awareness concerns, beginning teachers are given resources and training in the areas of classroom discipline, management and routines, and procedures aligned with the school's philosophy.

Beginning teachers are provided with written examples of rules, routines, and procedures for reference as they create a classroom management plan for the new classroom of students. Beginning teachers are provided time to be engaged in grand conversations with other peer buddies and mentors as to what procedures are expected in the classroom at the school site.

The novice needs guidance in establishing rules for the classroom that are aligned with school rules. Beginning teachers are not to be overwhelmed with managing the classroom but are provided quality examples to use to help establish a management plan for the classroom. Support from peer buddies, mentors, and coaches is necessary to assist the beginning teacher in establishing the rules, procedures, and routines in his or her classroom to make for a smooth school year.

Informational Concerns

Through group discussions about classroom management, sharing among beginning teachers within their grade level is initiated. Beginning teachers may visit teachers in other classrooms at the school site (or possibly other schools) who teach within the same grade level to observe how various classrooms are managed as well as how discipline and routines are established.

To fully assist with informational concerns, information is presented to the beginning teacher in an enthusiastic manner and is not intended to overwhelm the beginning teacher. Other faculty share written classroom management plan examples and allow the beginning teacher to model his or her classroom from a variety of the other plans being used at the school.

Personal Concerns

Beginning teachers express personal concerns regarding new classroom dynamics, and managing classroom behaviors while establishing workable routines and rules frequently becomes a daunting task. New teachers need to feel validated for their personal concerns, and they need opportunities to communicate their struggles, frustrations, and wants directly. The administration and collaboration team show that they are available to assist the beginning teacher with his or her classroom management needs throughout the day and school year.

The peer buddies collaborate with the beginning teacher on management ideas that have been successfully implemented in their classrooms. The peer buddies discuss with the beginning teacher the most effective management and discipline ideas for the school site. Pairing the novice's ideas about classroom management with a more experienced expert's ideas provides for a rich conversation in a supportive setting.

The beginning teacher is provided with a risk-free environment to ask for assistance and support from other faculty members in areas of classroom management. Understanding that the new teacher may feel inadequate or unprepared, the mentors and peer buddies offer support and guidance when needed to create and maintain a cohesive classroom structure.

Management Concerns

One of the most challenging areas of concern is management. The first step in assisting the beginning teacher with the most effective classroom management methods is to provide access to helpful resources such as videos, hard copies of other management plans, and school and district handbooks for students so that the beginning teacher can reference the rules already established. In addition, support incorporates ideas and plans for documenting behaviors, collecting data, and monitoring the effects of behavior interventions when they are utilized.

Desks and other student equipment including laptops or computers, classroom storage, materials, and supplies are provided for the beginning teacher so he or she can feel organized and able to set forth a system of management prior to the first day of school. Assisting the new teacher to arrange the classroom so that a positive environment is created will help get the first days off to a smooth start.

The beginning teacher submits a copy of his or her own classroom management plan, addressing all of the key components for the mentor and principal prior to the start of school for review so the collaboration team can be assured that the beginning teacher is prepared for his or her new class of students. The mentor and members of the collaboration team review the beginning teacher's plan of classroom management and arrangement and provide feedback.

Consequence Concerns

Beginning teachers are given release time to observe other classrooms within their subject or grade level to gain ideas and information about different approaches in classroom management. Observing others is an effective way to focus on consequence concerns. The beginning teachers are given time to share their new ideas with other grade levels or departments within the school or district. Beginning teachers use this release time to view various videos and attend beginning of the year seminars or workshops targeting those classroom management areas where they may need extra assistance.

Just like with subject and content concerns, the beginning teacher is concerned about the impact on students of guidance and disciplinary management plans. If behavior intervention plans are in place, the impact of these is also a concern. Providing an opportunity for the new teacher to express consequence concerns and receive positive affirming feedback is critical at this time.

Collaborative Concerns

Beginning teachers are given opportunities to attend training and professional development regarding effective classroom management within their grade level or content area. These trainings provide a better understanding of managing a classroom within the grade level in which the novice is teaching.

Beginning teachers are invited to collaborate with coaches and mentors on a regular basis to discuss the areas of management within their classroom that may or may not be working. Working with others in a positive collaborative environment gives collaborative concerns an affirming response.

Having time to process and identify areas that need bolstering with colleagues helps the new teacher develop as a partner with other teachers. If teachers share students, collaboration provides a way to seek common solutions.

Refocusing Concerns

Some beginning teachers come to the job with the idea that they already know the best methods for managing a classroom. The administration respects these individuals' ideas and provides ongoing support for them as a way to address refocusing concerns. The administration and collaboration team will continue to engage the beginning teacher in discussions about the latest and most effective methods of classroom management. Beginning teachers are given opportunities to share their own methods of classroom management while being immersed in various other effective strategies.

CONCERN OF THE ROLE OF A TEACHER AT THE SCHOOL AND WITHIN THE PROFESSION

Awareness Concerns

Beginning teachers express concern for the general expectations of teachers and the expectations as contributors to the teaching profession. Beginning teachers are given clear definitions and roles to refer to in order to adjust to the expectations of the school regarding the role of a teacher. These actions serve to allay awareness concerns. Beginning teachers are given ample opportunities to engage in conversations with other educators teaching at the school or within the district to help clearly define the roles for the beginning teacher in the classroom as well as in the profession.

Beginning teachers understand that they are to attend professional development trainings and workshops and even be willing to provide these types of trainings to other beginning teachers. Beginning teachers are less likely to be overwhelmed with their new position when they are provided with time and resources to further their education and level of understanding. Mentor teachers and coaches demonstrate professional development within the teaching community as a model for the beginning teacher to be continuously involved in furthering his or her development.

Informational Concerns

Group discussions regarding roles of the teacher within the climate of the school are initiated among the beginning teachers within their grade or subject levels as a way to work on informational concerns. A written description of the teacher's role at the school site is presented to the beginning teacher in an enthusiastic manner so as not to overwhelm the beginning teacher. The beginning teacher is provided with a copy of the roles of the teacher and is encouraged to ask questions and discuss the specifics of his or her job duties on a daily basis. The beginning teacher is also given resources for professional development opportunities throughout the school year as a means for furthering his or her training and education. The new teacher's role includes these actions:

- Observe mentor teachers
- Set goals
- Meet as a part of a collaboration team
- Journal with mentor
- Converse with peer buddy daily
- Listen and ask good questions
- Accept feedback and constructive criticism and be easily coachable and approachable
- Follow school and district rules and policies
- Be an example for your students

Personal Concerns

Beginning teachers express personal concern of the unknown. Being new to the profession, the novice may feel isolated or anxious about the move from being a candidate to becoming a fully employed teacher. These teachers need to feel validated for their concerns and be able to communicate their needs and wants directly to others who will listen attentively. The administration and collaboration team show that they are available to assist the beginning teacher with his or her needs throughout the day and school year. The peer buddies collaborate with the beginning teacher as to various teacher roles during the day.

Some key areas where teachers may need clarification about their role include parent-teacher conferences; special education referrals; duty at recess, before and after school, and at lunchtime; monitoring students in the hallway; addressing student behavior; and the teacher's role during the discipline process. The beginning teacher is provided with a risk-free environment to ask for assistance and support from other faculty members when discussing these and other topics.

Beginning teachers may express concern as to how to attend training and professional development. Beginning teachers will likely express concern on how best to report back to other faculty the findings they encountered during the training. Beginning teachers may feel intimidated to come back to a new faculty and attempt to share with them what they have learned at training seminars.

As a novice, the new teacher may decide to develop a deeper understanding of the profession by returning to school and pursuing additional degrees or certification. He or she may be unsure of the expectations of the first year of teaching and how much time would be available to keep up with graduate school work as well as effectively serve the classroom. Addressing these personal concerns will help the new teacher make informed decisions.

Management Concerns

The first step in assisting the beginning teacher with the management roles and responsibilities of his or her job is to provide access to many opportunities to discuss and share roles and duties within the school. The beginning teacher benefits from access to available resources to continue education and complete ongoing training so as to be able to share new and innovative methods of instruction with peers within the school building. Opportunities for leave time and early release are established for the beginning teacher to attend trainings and professional development to make for reachable goals of furthering his or her level of expertise.

Consequence Concerns

To address consequence concerns, beginning teachers are given release time to discuss with other faculty the roles and duties expected of them on a regular basis. Beginning teachers are provided with release time or professional days to attend workshops and training in areas of instructional practices. The beginning teacher is encouraged to return to the school and share what was learned with the rest of the faculty.

Providing time for beginning teachers to share their new ideas with other grade levels or departments within the school or district helps them develop into effective colleagues and professionals. As a contributor to the profession, the beginning teacher is encouraged to present new information and trainings to the faculty upon return to school as a way to grow professionally and as a leader in the teaching community.

Collaborative Concerns

Beginning teachers are given opportunities to attend training and professional development within their grade level or content area. These trainings provide a better understanding of the grade or curriculum in which they are teaching. District personnel and other experts are brought in to provide ongoing support and resources for the beginning teacher to utilize in his or her lesson instruction and further his or her training in the first few years of teaching.

New teachers are invited to share what they are implementing in the classroom at various faculty gatherings or meetings throughout the school year within their school setting or throughout the district. By sharing and engaging in discourse about high-quality teaching, collaborative concerns are effectively addressed.

Refocusing Concerns

As they enter a new school, novices will most likely come with numerous ideas and beliefs about the role they will assume. These ideas represent a compilation of experiences the new teacher has. The administration addresses refocusing concerns by demonstrating respect for individual ideas while providing ongoing support and copies of the roles of the teacher for reference. The administration and collaboration team encourage beginning teachers to express their concerns about various roles and duties in discussions within teams and with peer buddies as situations arise.

Novices may have just graduated and may not be interested in going to graduate school, attending more training, or participating in professional development opportunities. Presenting additional professional development ideas as leadership and growth opportunities may help the new teacher with refocusing concerns. The beginning teacher could also be invited to return to the faculty after such trainings and teach the others what was learned.

After a couple of years in a new teacher mentoring program, the fully supported new teacher is developing into an effective and fully integrated faculty member. In the third year of implementation, the beginning teacher is paired with a new beginning teacher who needs mentoring. At this time, the beginning teacher in his or her third year of teaching takes on the role of peer buddy to the new teacher. This makes for the continuation of the cycle of support from teacher to teacher, thus adding to the responsibility of the teacher to his or her profession.

KEY POINTS

Chapter five aligns CBAM with addressing concerns for beginning teachers as they participate in a mentoring program. By suggesting possible ways to address the new teacher's concerns at each of the seven levels of concern, this chapter addresses the areas of curriculum, classroom management, and the professional role as a new teacher at the school and within the profession. This chapter offers ideas regarding how to address any needs or concerns the new teacher may experience as he or she goes through the first year as a participant in the mentoring program.

Chapter Six

Addressing Concerns for Mentor Teachers

In chapter five, new teacher concerns were identified and ideas for meeting them were suggested at each of the seven stages of concern. Just as Hall and Hord's Stages of Concern (2006) is recommended for use with new teachers, it is also recommended for addressing mentor teachers' concerns. Mentor teachers serve in a very different role, yet their concerns follow a similar developmental progression. In this chapter each of the levels will be discussed and ideas will be presented for consideration with basic explanations of individual concerns in the varying phases of the developmental process of the new teacher mentoring plan. Below are the stages of concern for the mentor in the order in which they are to be presented.

Stage 0—Awareness Concerns

- If possible, involve mentor teachers in discussions and decisions about the innovation and its implementation.
- Share enough information to arouse interest, but not so much that it overwhelms.
- Acknowledge that a lack of awareness is expected and reasonable, and that no questions about the innovation are foolish.
- Encourage unaware persons to talk with colleagues who know about the innovation.
- Take steps to minimize gossip and inaccurate sharing of information about the innovation.

Stage 1—Informational Concerns

- Provide clear and accurate information about the mentoring process and expectations of the mentor.
- Use a variety of ways to share information—verbally, in writing, and through any available media. Communicate with mentors and with small and large groups.
- Have persons who have used the innovation in other settings visit with your teachers. Visits to other schools can also be arranged.
- Help mentor teachers see how the innovation relates to their current practices, both in regard to similarities and differences.
- Be enthusiastic and enhance the visibility of others who are excited.

Stage 2—Personal Concerns

- Legitimize the existence and expression of mentors' personal concerns. Knowing these concerns are common and that others have them can be comforting.
- Use personal notes and conversations to provide encouragement and reinforce personal adequacy.
- Connect these mentor teachers with other mentors across the school district whose personal concerns have diminished and who will be supportive.
- Show how the innovation can be implemented sequentially rather than in one big leap. It is important to establish expectations that are attainable.
- Do not push innovation use, but encourage and support it while maintaining expectations.

Stage 3—Management Concerns

- Clarify the steps and components of the mentoring process and expectations. Information from innovation configurations will be helpful here.
- Provide answers that address the small and specific "how-to" issues that are so often the cause of management concerns.
- Demonstrate exact and practical solutions to the logistical problems that contribute to the concerns.
- Help teachers sequence specific activities and set timelines for their accomplishments.
- Attend to the immediate demands of the innovation, not what will be or can be in the future.

Stage 4—Consequence Concerns

- Provide mentors with opportunities to visit other mentoring settings where the innovation is in use and to attend conferences on the topic.
- Don't overlook mentors. Provide them with positive feedback and needed support.
- Find opportunities for the mentors to share their skills with other mentors and other teachers in the profession.
- Share information with mentors pertaining to the innovation.

Stage 5—Collaborative Concerns

- Provide mentors with opportunities to develop those skills necessary for working collaboratively.
- Bring together mentors from both within and outside the school who are interested in collaboration.
- Help these mentor collaborators establish reasonable expectations and timelines for the collaborative effort.
- Use these mentors to provide technical assistance to others who need assistance.
- Encourage the collaborators, but don't attempt to force collaboration on those mentors who are not interested.

Stage 6—Refocusing Concerns

- Respect and encourage the interest mentors have for finding a better way.
- Help mentors channel their ideas and energies in ways that will be productive rather than counterproductive.
- Encourage mentors to act on their concerns for program improvement.
- Help mentors access resources they may need to refine their ideas and put them into practice.

CONCERN OF KNOWLEDGE OF CURRICULUM AND SUBJECT MATTER

Awareness Concerns

Mentor teachers sometimes enter this new partnership expressing general concern upon receiving their new mentoring assignment with only knowledge of their own subject matter. Some mentors bring a wealth of experience in a variety of grade levels and instructional settings while others may be extremely seasoned in one or two content areas or grades. Regardless, a highly helpful mentor will bring a wide array of knowledge and skills to assist the novice.

Mentor teachers need to be given access to resources and trainings, regardless of their prior experiences, that can provide the curriculum and information for them to learn, review, or revisit in order to mentor and assist their protégés. To develop increased awareness, mentor teachers are given access to the state standards, district guides, teacher guides, other materials, and anything else they may need. A rule of thumb: if a new teacher receives access to materials, the mentor also needs the same materials.

Mentor teachers engage in focused conversations with other mentor teachers within their same subject or grade level about the timeline of the curriculum for the school year in order to best support their protégés. Long-range plans and any other related materials that are needed are readily accessible to the mentor teachers.

To keep mentor teachers from being overwhelmed with this new task, they are provided with time and resources to become knowledgeable of the curriculum and information they will present to the beginning teacher. Support from other mentors within a network is established during this time and mentor teachers are able to identify those fellow veteran teachers who are capable and willing to assist them through this process.

Informational Concerns

Group discussions about the curriculum among the mentor teachers within their grade or subject levels are encouraged. Just as technological resources are provided to the new teacher, they also are provided to mentors along with other materials regarding content. Mentor teachers may visit the classrooms of other mentor teachers at the school site as well as classrooms of mentor teachers who teach within the same content or grade levels at other schools in order to ask questions, borrow materials, and observe how the curriculum and content is presented in various ways. Understanding that the mentor is in a new situation just as is the novice, information is presented to the mentor teacher in a positive enthusiastic manner that invites and does not overwhelm.

Personal Concerns

Just like novice teachers, mentor teachers will likely express personal concerns of the unknown. Mentors may be uncertain about the demands placed upon them by the program, so reassurance is needed. These more seasoned teachers need to feel validated for their concerns and should be able to communicate their needs and wants directly to their school leaders.

Administrators and the collaboration team will be called upon to show that they are available to assist mentor teachers with their needs throughout the school year. Other mentor teachers on the campus may also be called upon to collaborate about ideas that may have worked in their classrooms while planning for instruction.

The mentor solicits new ideas and plans that would assist the beginning teacher to plan his or her own lessons. The mentor teacher is provided with a risk-free environment to ask for assistance and support from other faculty and administrative members. Mentors will also need opportunities to express their content and curriculum needs in a supportive environment.

Sometimes these concerns are very personal, as the committed mentor wants his or her novice to be successful in the classroom. The new teacher may be viewed as another student to support, and this will need to be recognized.

Management Concerns

One of the first considerations for the mentor regarding his or her management concerns is assisting him or her with easy access to all of the materials needed to assist the protégé or new teacher to be able to plan quality lessons. The mentor will need necessary technology and teacher resources, including all materials that have been provided to the novice.

Sometimes, a mentor's array of materials may be less up to date than the new teacher's, so it is critical that this be checked and adjusted as needed. The mentor teacher will need to be knowledgeable of the beginning teacher's deadlines for submitting lesson plans as well as the required components of the school's or district's lesson plans. Managing one's own classroom while offering guidance to a new teacher can be a daunting task for the mentor.

It is important to provide both mentor and novice any and all opportunities to avail themselves of management tools, including professional development, outside assistance, or software. By recognizing and meeting the management needs and concerns of the mentor, the new teacher continues to learn about community, asking for and receiving high-quality assistance.

Consequence Concerns

Mentor teachers are given release time to observe the classrooms of the new teachers that they are mentoring as well as to observe other mentor teachers within their subject or grade level to gain ideas and information about different approaches in instruction. These mentor teachers are given time to share their new ideas with other mentor teachers in their grade level or department within the school or district.

Mentors will have consequence concerns about the impact of their work on the new teachers as well as their own students, so this possible concern will need recognition and attention. Time used for mentorship may have an impact on the mentor's other duties, so an understanding administration will ensure that this concern is addressed through conversation.

Collaborative Concerns

Mentor teachers are given opportunities to attend trainings and needed professional development within their grade level or content area. These trainings should provide a better understanding of the mentoring process and how to best service the beginning teacher. District personnel such as curriculum coaches, mentor trainers, and other experts are brought in to provide ongoing support and resources that are related to their area of expertise for the mentor teacher to utilize in his or her assistance and support of the beginning teacher.

Mentor teachers are invited to collaborate with these coaches and trainers on a regular basis to reinforce what they are working on with the new teacher in his or her classroom. As each mentor–new teacher relationship develops and grows, ongoing opportunities for the mentors to collaborate with others regarding curricular changes and how to assist the new teacher will be needed. Witnessing a true collaborative environment is perhaps one of the best experiences that a new teacher can have.

Refocusing Concerns

When mentor teachers accept a mentoring role, some may come with preconceived ideas about what they already know about how best to support the new teacher regarding content and its delivery. With years of experience, mentors provide a wealth and depth of knowledge, and their role as mentors speaks to this knowledge.

Savvy administrators respect these individual ideas and support the knowledge mentors bring, but also provide ongoing support and innovative methods of instruction that are available. The administration and collaboration team encourage mentor teachers to express concerns about the content knowledge in discussions with other mentors and with the team. Mentor teachers are given ample opportunities to share their own knowledge of the content and how to best support and exemplify appropriate planning and implementation of the lessons to the beginning teacher.

CONCERN OF CLASSROOM MANAGEMENT

Awareness Concerns

Perhaps more than in any other area, mentor teachers will have concerns with the beginning teacher's basic management of students, discipline, and arranging of the classroom. Mentor teachers are given needed resources on how to assist and support new teachers in the areas of classroom discipline, management, routines, and procedures that are aligned with the school's philosophy and mission.

Mentor teachers assist their protégés by providing them with written examples of rules, routines, and procedures to reference while creating a classroom management plan for the new classroom of students. Sometimes mentors may need gentle reminding about the importance of helping the new teacher reflect on what is and is not working rather than telling the new teacher how to manage the classroom.

Reflection honors the novice teacher's attempts and developing skills in classroom management. The mentor stands ready as a safety net and more seasoned expert to help the new teacher see and adjust procedures and processes.

Mentor teachers are engaged in targeted conversations with other mentors about what procedures are expected of the new teacher in the classroom at the school site. Mentor teachers need guidance in assisting the beginning teacher when they begin establishing rules for the classroom that are aligned with schoolwide rules.

Mentor teachers are not to be overwhelmed with assisting the beginning teacher with the management of their own classroom but are instead to be provided resources and quality examples to use to help the beginning teacher with this. Support from coaches, administration, and other mentors is needed to assist the beginning teacher in establishing the rules, procedures, and routines in his or her classroom to make for a smooth start to the school year.

Informational Concerns

Mentor teachers share classroom management strategies with other mentor teachers in their grade level through group discussions. Mentor teachers may visit other teachers' classrooms at the school site as well as other schools with mentors in the same grade level or subject area to observe how various classrooms are managed as well as how discipline and routines are established in order to best inform the new teacher.

Other mentors can share written classroom management plan examples that the mentor can share with the beginning teacher and allow him or her to model his or her classroom from a variety of the other plans being used at the school. It is of utmost importance to address informational concerns through the timely provision of resources to both mentor and novice. Mentors may get frustrated when needed information is not readily accessible.

Personal Concerns

Mentor teachers will express personal concerns of the unknown in classroom management just as with content and curriculum. A mentor may wonder if a beginning teacher is up to the challenge of assisting a new teacher, especially if the new teacher expresses personal or other concerns about classroom management.

Providing sincere validation for the mentor teachers' concerns and offering opportunities to communicate their needs and areas of struggle are a critical part of an administrator's responsibilities. The administration and collaboration team show that they are available to assist the mentor teacher with his or her needs throughout the school year.

Other mentors within the school and school district collaborate with the mentor teacher on management ideas that are based on best practices and effectiveness. The mentor teacher is provided with a risk-free environment to ask for assistance and support from other faculty members in areas of assisting the beginning teacher in his or her own classroom management.

Management Concerns

The management concerns of mentors may take several forms. These include keeping up with the mentor's own responsibilities while assisting the novice. They might consist of helping a new teacher develop classroom procedures while establishing the mentor's procedures and using similar or even different processes.

The mentor may have concerns regarding how classroom management ideas should be communicated with the beginning teacher. Mentors need time to reflect, observe, and provide feedback while also receiving support for their own classrooms in whatever ways are needed. One supportive gesture is providing access to videos, hard copies of other management plans, and also school and district handbooks for students so that the beginning teacher can reference the processes already established.

Desks and other student equipment including laptops or computers, classroom storage, materials, and supplies are provided for the beginning teacher so he or she can feel organized and able to set forth a system of management prior to the first day of school. This keeps the mentor from having to advocate for the new teacher, which may take away from the mentor's own preparation efforts.

After a plan development period, the beginning teacher submits a copy of his or her own classroom management plan addressing all of the key components to the mentor and principal prior to the start of school so the collaboration team can be assured that the beginning teacher is prepared for his or her new class of students.

Consequence Concerns

Mentor teachers are concerned about the time it takes to gather the most pertinent information to assist a beginning teacher with classroom management. Consequence concerns may go hand in hand with management concerns. While being focused on managing all the relevant tasks, the mentor may also struggle with the consequences of underperforming or not getting all the pieces put in place.

As needed, mentor teachers are given release time to observe other classroom teachers within their subject or grade level to gain ideas and information as to different approaches in providing feedback to new teachers in areas such as classroom management. While time is provided, the savvy administrator ensures that the time is quality time and that both mentor and teacher have support for their own classrooms while they are focused on classroom management issues.

Mentors also use time to attend beginning of the year seminars or workshops targeting those areas where they may need extra information in order to help and support the beginning teachers in their classrooms. Attending with the new teacher, other mentors, or both can provide a way to alleviate consequence concerns.

Collaborative Concerns

A recurring theme is finding adequate time to establish a new mentoring program. Mentor teachers will likely express concerns regarding being allowed time for training and collaboration during this mentoring process. Mentor teachers are given opportunities to attend professional development activities that focus on classroom management issues where time is given for collaboration with others regarding how best to support the new teacher.

These opportunities provide a better understanding of supporting a new teacher in such areas as managing a classroom within the grade level in which he or she is teaching. It stands to reason that the mentor will also need time to collaborate with coaches and other mentors on a regular basis to discuss the areas of needed support and information in order to best assist the new teacher.

Refocusing Concerns

Some mentor teachers, through their relationships with new teachers and the collaboration team, may develop new ideas for improving systems of classroom management for both the classroom and the school. Their own skill may be significantly strengthened through the mentoring relationship. Administrators respect these individuals' ideas and provide ongoing support for them.

The administration and collaboration team continue to engage the mentor teacher in discussions within mentoring teams and with peer buddies on new and effective methods of assisting new teachers with classroom management. Mentor teachers are given opportunities to share their own methods of assisting new teachers with classroom management while being immersed in various other effective strategies.

CONCERN OF THE ROLE AS A MENTOR TEACHER AT THE SCHOOL AND WITHIN THE PROFESSION

Awareness Concerns

Mentor teachers express concern regarding general expectations as a mentor teacher and a professional contributor to the profession. Mentor teachers are given clear definitions and roles to refer to in order to adjust to the expectations of the school in their roles as mentor teachers. Mentor teachers are given opportunities to engage in conversations with other educators teaching and mentoring at the school or within the district to help clearly define the roles of the beginning teacher in the classroom as well as in the profession. Mentor teachers are willing to learn and attend mentoring professional development trainings and workshops and are also willing to provide these types of trainings to other new mentor teachers.

Mentor teachers are not overwhelmed with their new position and are provided with time and resources to further their education and trainings. Mentor teachers and coaches are able to demonstrate professional development within the teaching community as a model for the beginning teacher to be continuously involved in furthering his or her education and training.

Informational Concerns

Group discussions regarding roles of the mentor teacher within the climate of the school are initiated among other mentor teachers within their grade or subject levels. All information or written descriptions of the mentor teacher's role at the school site are presented to the mentor teacher in a supportive manner and are not intended to overwhelm the mentor teacher.

The beginning mentor teacher is provided with a copy of the roles of the mentor teacher and is encouraged to ask questions and discuss the specifics of his or her job duties on a daily basis. The mentor teacher is given resources for professional development opportunities throughout the school year as a means for furthering his or her mentor training and education. The mentor roles include the following:

- Observe
- Set goals
- Set up time to assist while beginning teacher goes to observe
- Provide quality lessons for observation
- Journal with beginning teacher
- Model appropriate professionalism
- Demonstrate appropriate contact with parents
- Listen and be supportive
- Provide encouragement
- Provide feedback and other ideas and methods of instruction
- Provide resources

Personal Concerns

Mentor teachers express personal concern of the unknown, especially if they are new to the mentoring role. Typically, a mentor is chosen for his or her value and contributions to the profession, yet personal concerns may still persist. These teachers need to feel validated for their concerns and be able to communicate their needs and wants directly. The administration and collaboration team show that they are available to assist the mentor teacher with his or her needs throughout the school year.

Some key areas in which mentor teachers may need clarification on their roles may include assisting the new teacher with parent-teacher conferences; special education referrals; duty at recess, before and after school; and at lunchtime; monitoring students in the hallway; determining misbehavior of students; and the teacher's role during the discipline process. The mentor teacher is provided with a risk-free environment to ask for assistance and support from other faculty members and fellow mentors when discussing these and other topics.

Mentor teachers express personal concerns as to how they can become involved in mentor professional development as well as how to report back to the faculty what they learned during training. Mentor teachers express questions and interest in returning back to school to achieve a higher degree or additional certification but are unsure of the expectations of the mentor teacher and how much time would be available for them to keep up with graduate school work in addition to fulfilling their roles as mentor teachers.

Management Concerns

The first step in assisting the mentor teacher with the roles and responsibilities of his or her job is to provide access to many opportunities to discuss and share roles and duties within the school. The mentor teacher benefits from access resources that are available to continue education and complete ongoing training so as to be able to share new and innovative methods of instruction with peers and new teachers within the school building. Opportunities for leave time and early release are established for the mentor teacher to attend trainings and professional development to make for reachable goals of furthering their level of expertise.

Consequence Concerns

Mentor teachers are given release time to discuss the roles and duties that are expected of them with other mentors on the faculty. Consequence concerns may occur as a result of the new responsibilities, and a mentor may wonder about the impact of his or her efforts on the new teacher, the mentor himself or herself, the school, or even the profession.

Mentor teachers are provided with release time or professional days to attend workshops and training in areas of instructional practices. The mentor teacher is encouraged to return to the school and share what was learned with the rest of the faculty. These mentor teachers are given time to share their new ideas with other grade levels or departments within the school or district. As a contributor to the profession, the mentor teacher is encouraged to present new information and trainings to the faculty upon return to school as a way to grow professionally and as a leader in the teaching community.

Collaborative Concerns

Mentor teachers may express concerns related to the need for collaboration time with other mentors in the school or across the district. Mentors are given opportunities to attend training and professional development within their grade level or content area to allow for such collaboration. These trainings provide a better understanding of the grade or curriculum in which mentors are teaching.

District personnel and other experts may be brought in to provide ongoing mentor support and resources for the mentor teacher to utilize in his or her lesson instruction and to further his or her ability to model and support beginning teachers. With each professional development opportunity, mentors need time to coordinate, cooperate, and collaborate with others in order to strengthen their own understanding and to have their voices heard.

Refocusing Concerns

Some mentor teachers enter the job with the idea that they already know their role as a teacher at the school site, the district, or the profession. As they mature in their role working with new teachers, mentors may have ideas that improve the new teacher mentoring program. Administrators respect and support these individual ideas but also provide ongoing support and the latest copies of the roles of the mentor teacher for the mentor teachers' reference.

The administrator provides a digital copy of the mentoring book for the mentor teachers to refer to throughout the school year as the need arises. The administration and collaboration team encourage the mentor teachers to express their concerns about various roles and duties in discussions. Mentor contributions should be reflected in new teacher resources.

In the third year of implementation the mentor teacher may be partnered up with a new mentor who needs training and support to be a mentor to a new teacher. At this time the mentor teacher may become a peer buddy to the new mentor teacher. This makes for the continuation of the cycle of support from mentor to mentor, thus adding to the responsibility of the teacher to his or her profession.

KEY POINTS

Chapter six aligns CBAM with addressing concerns for the mentor teacher as he or she takes on their role within a mentoring program. This chapter addresses the concerns of curriculum, classroom management, and the professional role for mentor teachers at the school and within the profession.

This chapter explains how to address the mentor's concerns as he or she goes through the first year of serving as a mentor to a new teacher. As mentors strengthen their understanding and performance in the role, their ideas and contributions are reflected in the new teacher mentoring program.

Chapter Seven

Addressing Concerns for Curriculum Coaches

Curriculum coach concerns are also addressed using Hall and Hord's Stages of Concern (2006). It is recognized that not all districts and schools use curriculum coaches or instructional facilitators, but for those who incorporate such roles into their mentoring program, concerns will likely emerge.

These concerns are later addressed in this section of the guide with basic explanations of each individual concern in the varying phases of the developmental process of the plan. The term *curriculum coach* will be used to represent both curriculum coach and instructional facilitator. Below are the stages of concern for the coach/facilitator in the order in which they are to be presented:

Stage 0—Awareness Concerns

- If possible, involve coaches in discussions and decisions about the innovation and its implementation.
- Share enough information to arouse interest, but not so much that it overwhelms.
- Acknowledge that a lack of awareness is expected and reasonable, and that no questions about the innovation are foolish.
- Encourage unaware persons to talk with colleagues who know about the innovation.
- Take steps to minimize gossip and inaccurate sharing of information about the innovation.

Stage 1—Informational Concerns

- Provide clear and accurate information about the coaching process and expectations of the coach.
- Use a variety of ways to share information—verbally, in writing, and through any available media. Communicate with coaches and with small and large groups.
- Have persons who have used the innovation in other settings visit with your teachers. Visits to other schools can also be arranged.
- Help coaches see how the innovation relates to their current practices, both in regard to similarities and differences.
- Be enthusiastic and enhance the visibility of others who are excited.

Stage 2—Personal Concerns

- Legitimize the existence and expression of coaches' personal concerns. Knowing these concerns are common and that others have them can be comforting.
- Use personal notes and conversations to provide encouragement and reinforce personal adequacy.
- Connect these coaches with other coaches across the school district whose personal concerns have diminished and who will be supportive.
- Show how the innovation can be implemented sequentially rather than in one big leap. It is important to establish expectations that are attainable.
- Do not push innovation use, but encourage and support it while maintaining expectations.

Stage 3—Management Concerns

- Clarify the steps and components of the mentoring process and expectations. Information from innovation configurations will be helpful here.
- Provide answers that address the small and specific "how-to" issues that are so often the cause of management concerns.
- Demonstrate exact and practical solutions to the logistical problems that contribute to the concerns.
- Help teachers sequence specific activities and set timelines for their accomplishments.
- Attend to the immediate demands of the innovation, not what will be or can be in the future.

Stage 4—Consequence Concerns

- Provide coaches with opportunities to visit other mentoring settings where the innovation is in use and to attend conferences on the topic.
- Don't overlook these coaches. Provide them with positive feedback and needed support.
- Find opportunities for the coaches to share their skills with other coaches and other teachers in the profession.
- Share with these coaches information pertaining to the innovation.

Stage 5—Collaborative Concerns

- Provide coaches with opportunities to develop those skills necessary for working collaboratively.
- Bring together coaches, both within and outside the school, who are interested in collaboration.
- Help these coaching collaborators establish reasonable expectations and timelines for the collaborative effort.
- Use these persons to provide technical assistance to others who need assistance.
- Encourage the collaborators, but don't attempt to force collaboration on those coaches who are not interested.

Stage 6—Refocusing Concerns

- Respect and encourage the interest these coaches have for finding a better way.
- Help coaches channel their ideas and energies in ways that will be productive rather than counterproductive.
- Encourage these coaches to act on their concerns for program improvement.
- Help these coaches access resources they may need to refine their ideas and put them into practice.

CONCERN OF KNOWLEDGE OF CURRICULUM AND SUBJECT MATTER

Awareness Concerns

Curriculum or instructional coaches may express general concern upon receiving their new mentoring assignment. If a curriculum coach targets only one area such as math or language arts, he or she may be concerned about providing support in the remaining areas. Coaches may also be concerned about how mentors and new teachers will work within the framework of the curriculum.

Coaches are given access to the same resources and trainings provided to others in the team. Coaches may already have an array of materials, yet it is important that they be given access to any other curriculum materials they may need. Conversations with other coaches and mentor teachers about the scope and sequence or timeline of the curriculum implementation will need to take place.

Long-range plans are provided and any other materials that are needed are readily accessible to the coach. To prevent the coaches from being overwhelmed with this new task, time and resources are provided to strengthen knowledge of the curriculum and other mentor information. Support from the administration as well as other coaches within a network is established during this time. Coaches are able to identify those fellow veteran teachers who are capable and utilize them throughout this process.

Informational Concerns

Group discussions among the coaches about the curriculum within their grade or subject levels are initiated. Generally, curriculum coaches are responsible for guiding their schools or districts through curricular issues, and adding information about a new mentoring program may call for time to process and assimilate program elements. Technological resources are provided as well as other curriculum materials.

Coaches visit classrooms of other participating coaches, mentor teachers at the school site, and mentors and coaches from other schools teaching within the same content areas. Coaches are encouraged to ask questions, borrow materials, and develop a broad view of how the curriculum and content are presented throughout the district.

Personal Concerns

Coaches express personal concerns of the unknown aspects of any curriculum changes, although generally this is an area of strength for the coach or facilitator. Coaches need to feel validated for their concerns and be able to communicate their needs and wants directly. One coach may be responsible for numerous teacher concerns including working with the mentor and new teacher. The administration and collaboration team show that they are available to assist the coach with his or her needs throughout the day and school year.

Other coaches on the campus collaborate with each other on ideas that may have worked in their settings while planning and leading content and curriculum discussions. Coaches often use a variety of methods for helping teachers implement curriculum, and they may be concerned about the effect new responsibilities may have on them.

The coach solicits new ideas and plans that would assist the mentor and beginning teacher to plan their own lessons. Roles will need to be clarified and conversations will need to take place among coach, mentor, and new teacher. The coach is provided with a risk-free environment to ask for assistance and support from other faculty and administrative members.

Management Concerns

Instructional coaches may express concerns about efficiency, organization, and scheduling time to meet with other team members and strengthen their own skills. Scheduling observations and consultations with numerous individuals takes administrative support, time, and opportunity. Establishing the mentoring program as a priority and clearly providing structure can help address the coaches' management concerns.

A laptop or computer is provided for research and instruction along with hard copies and online versions of teacher resources. The coach is knowledgeable of the school's or district's lesson plan requirements as well as the timeline for submitting lesson plans to the administration.

Consequence Concerns

Coaches are given release time to observe and consult with the new teacher and mentor whom they are coaching as well as observe other coaches, mentors, or other veteran teachers within their subject or grade level. The coach may express concern about the level of commitment it takes to meet with and support so many other individuals.

Add to concern for level of commitment a concern for student outcomes, and the coach will likely contemplate his or her effectiveness in implementing change. Consequence concerns encompass an individual's focus on students within his or her sphere of influence, and the scope of the coach's work necessitates time and resources to affirm and support this critical role.

Collaborative Concerns

Coaches are given opportunities to attend any needed training and professional development within their areas of identified need. Ongoing discussion with others about how best to support the program provides a better understanding of the mentoring process and how to best serve the new teacher. Personnel such as district curriculum coaches, mentor trainers, and other experts will be brought in to provide ongoing support and resources that are currently related to their areas of expertise for the coach to utilize in assisting and supporting the new teacher. Coaches are invited and encouraged to collaborate with mentors and trainers on a regular basis to reinforce what they are working on with the mentor and new teacher in their classrooms.

Refocusing Concerns

In curriculum and knowledge of content, some coaches enter the role with the idea that they already know where the best information is and how to best support the mentors and beginning teachers within their school. Administrators respect these individual ideas and support coaches' methods of instruction, but also provide ongoing support and innovative resources that are readily available.

The administration and collaboration team encourage the coach to express his or her concerns about the content knowledge in discussions with other mentors or coaches. Coaches are given ample opportunities to share their own knowledge of the content and how to best support and exemplify appropriate planning and implementation of the lessons for the beginning teacher.

CONCERN OF CLASSROOM MANAGEMENT

Awareness Concerns

Coaches may also have concerns with the new teacher's basic managing and arranging of the classroom. This may or may not be a coach's area of emphasis, so coaches are given resources and training on how to assist and support new teachers in the areas of curriculum, classroom discipline, management, routines, and procedures that align with the school's philosophy and school-wide plan.

Coaches are able to pull from resources provided to them, including current trends, in order to best provide the mentor and beginning teacher with written examples of rules, routines, and procedures for them to reference as they create a classroom management plan for the new classroom of students. Coaches are engaged in conversations with other mentors and coaches as to which procedures are expected of the new teacher in the classroom at the school site and any needs they have.

Coaches need guidance in assisting the mentor and new teacher when they begin searching for literature to support establishing rules for the classroom that are aligned with the schoolwide rules. Coaches are not to be overwhelmed with assisting the mentor and new teacher with this, but are provided resources to share with the mentor and new teacher on quality examples to use to help establish a management plan for the classroom. Support from coaches, administration, and other mentors is needed to assist the beginning teacher in establishing the rules, procedures, and routines in the classroom to make for a smooth start to the school year.

Informational Concerns

Coaches and mentor teachers at the same grade levels share through group discussions about classroom management. Coaches may visit other teacher's classrooms at the school site as well as possibly other schools to gather information that may help the mentor or new teacher.

The coach may need more information about general issues of classroom management to serve more effectively in his or her role. If the coach specializes more in issues of curriculum, interest in classroom management may be more related to general characteristics, effects, and details of implementation. Coaches also share any new information learned about classroom management with the mentor and beginning teacher.

Personal Concerns

Coaches express personal concern of the unknown, especially if this is not their area of focus. They need to feel validated for their concerns and able to communicate these directly. The administration and collaboration team show that they are available to assist the coach with his or her needs throughout the school year.

The coaches within the school and school district collaborate with the mentor teacher on management ideas that have been deemed effective. The coach is provided with a risk-free environment to ask for assistance and support from other faculty members in areas of assisting the mentor and new teacher in their own classroom management.

Management Concerns

A coach will need access to the same materials regarding classroom management (online resources, professional development, hard copies of management plans, etc.) and also school and district handbooks for students in order to provide support to both the mentor and new teacher. Management concerns will likely involve how the coach can best utilize resources to provide support to others in the mentoring program.

Technology and other equipment including laptops or tablets, classroom storage, materials, and supplies are provided for the coach so he or she can feel organized and able to provide positive classroom management techniques throughout the school year. Sometimes what is needed most from the coach is a listening ear for the mentor and new teacher while they work on establishing classroom routines, procedures, and management plans.

Consequence Concerns

Coaches are generally deeply concerned about student impact and student outcomes. As content experts, coaches will be familiar with data, trends, assessment results, and other information about students. Classroom management issues can impact student outcomes directly or indirectly. Coaches will pay close attention to the new teacher's implementation of all classroom components, and will be aware of classroom management, procedures, rules, and the degree to which these are successful.

A coach may be in a good position to provide reflective feedback to both mentor and new teacher. Coaches may wish to observe other coaching strategies as well as other mentor teachers within their subject or grade level to gain ideas and information as to different approaches in providing feedback regarding areas such as classroom management. Coaches need time to share their ideas with other members of the team, including the new teacher and mentor.

Collaborative Concerns

Coaches also need to be given opportunities to attend training and professional development regarding classroom management in order to stay abreast of policies, trends, procedures, etc. Professional development opportunities provide a better understanding of supporting a beginning teacher and mentor in such areas as managing a classroom.

Coaches are invited to collaborate with other mentors and coaches on a regular basis to discuss the areas of needed support and information in order to best assist the new teacher. Coaches can facilitate conversations, provide feedback, and suggest resources through collaborative relationships.

Refocusing Concerns

Coaches are in a good position to provide an extra set of hands, eyes, and ears as well as suggest ideas for strengthening systems that are already in place. Because coaches see a wide variety of classroom implementation structures, they may be key persons to help the mentor and new teacher seek powerful new alternatives to existing processes.

Sometimes, a coach may come to the job with the idea that they already know the best methods for working with the mentor and beginning teacher in the classroom. Administrators respect these individual ideas and provide ongoing support for them. The administration and collaboration team continue to engage the coach in discussions on new and effective methods of assisting beginning teachers with classroom management. Coaches are given opportunities to share their own methods of classroom management while being immersed in various other effective strategies.

CONCERN OF THE ROLE AS A COACH AT THE SCHOOL AND WITHIN THE PROFESSION

Awareness Concerns

Coaches express concern for the general expectations of them as contributors to the profession. Generally coaches are former classroom teachers who have distinguished themselves in the classroom. They may have even served in other mentoring roles. With the new mentoring program, coaches are given clear definitions and roles to refer to in order to adjust to any different expectations in the role as a coach.

Coaches are provided with opportunities to engage in conversations with other educators who may be teaching and/or mentoring at the school or district to help clearly define their roles as coaches. Coaches understand that not only should they be willing to attend coaching and mentoring professional development trainings and workshops, but they should also provide these types of trainings to other new mentor teachers.

To assist the coach in any added responsibilities, they are provided with time and resources to further their education and training. Coaches and mentor teachers demonstrate professional development within the teaching community as a model for the beginning teacher to be continuously involved in furthering his or her education and training.

Informational Concerns

Collaborative discussions regarding roles of the coach within the school are initiated with mentor teachers and other stakeholders. The information or written description of the coach's role at the school site is discussed or even co-constructed with the coach. The beginning teacher is provided with a copy of the role of the coach and is encouraged to ask questions and provide feedback regularly. The coach is provided resources and opportunities for professional development throughout the school year as a means of furthering training and education. The coach's roles include the following:

- Provide support and counsel
- Set up time to visit regularly
- Provide curriculum resources
- Provide ideas for professional development and furthering education
- Model appropriate professionalism
- Listen and be supportive
- Provide encouragement
- Provide feedback

- Assist with paperwork, centers, instruction, and other daily duties of the beginning teacher

Personal Concerns

Coaches may express personal concerns regarding their contributions to the profession. As with other areas, a coach may need to feel validated for his or her concerns and be able to communicate these. Even the best coaches may sometimes express uncertainty about their adequacy in supporting the new teacher. The administration and collaboration team show that they are available to assist the coach with his or her needs.

Some key areas where coaches may need clarification include assisting the new teacher with curriculum; parent-teacher conferences; special education referrals; duty at recess, before and after school, and at lunchtime; monitoring students in the hallway; understanding challenging behaviors of students; and the teacher's role during the discipline process. The coach is provided with a risk-free environment to ask for assistance and support from other faculty members and fellow mentors when discussing these and other topics.

Coaches express concern as to how they can engage in training and professional development as well as how to share new information. Coaches are invited to share in their experiences with the other members of the collaboration team as well as other faculty members in an effort to increase overall organizational knowledge of best practices. Coaches express questions and interest in achieving a higher degree but may be unsure of the expectations of this new role.

Management Concerns

An instructional coach will need many opportunities to discuss and share roles and duties within the school. The coach benefits from access to resources that are available to continue developing his or her depth of knowledge in order to share new and innovative methods of instruction with peers and new teachers within the school building. Opportunities for leave time and early release are established for the coach to attend trainings and professional development to deepen his or her level of expertise.

Consequence Concerns

Coaches are given release time to discuss roles and duties and participate in other activities designed to strengthen the new mentor program. Here, as in other areas, the coach may be concerned about the impact on students as a result of any intervention implementation, including the mentoring program.

To ensure a positive impact of the work engaged in by coaches, opportunities for sharing their expertise are provided. As a contributor to the profession, the coach is encouraged to present evidence-based practices and other relevant information to the faculty as a way to grow professionally and as a leader in the teaching community.

Collaborative Concerns

A coach is perhaps one of the best members of the collaboration team because of the very nature of their position. A coach cheers, assists, supports, and guides in order to implement change and achieve desired goals. Coaches are collaborators and coordinators and by their very nature serve to contribute greatly to the profession. In order to be most effective, a coach needs opportunities to work with others in the creation and implementation of a new teacher mentoring program.

Refocusing Concerns

The attentive coach will quickly begin to identify ways to improve and enhance the mentoring program. Administrators respect these individual ideas and support them while providing ongoing support through collaboration. The administration and collaboration team encourage the coach to express innovative ideas about various roles and duties in discussions.

In the third year of implementation the coach is assigned to mentor a new coach who needs training and support to coach beginning teachers. At this time the veteran coach becomes a mentor to the new coach. This makes for the continuation of the cycle of support from coach to coach, thus adding to the responsibility of the teacher to his or her profession.

KEY POINTS

Chapter seven aligns CBAM with addressing concerns for instructional coaches of beginning teachers as they become involved in a mentoring program. This chapter addresses the concerns a coach may have about the curriculum being taught, classroom management utilized by the new teacher, and the overall professional role of a curriculum coach within the profession. This chapter explains how to address any needs or concerns the coach may experience as he or she coaches a new teacher and supports the new teacher's mentor within a mentoring program.

Chapter Eight

Addressing Concerns for Peer Buddies

The mentoring program incorporates assistance from other members of the faculty to include additional support for the beginning teacher. Peer buddies can be other members of the faculty who are willing to provide ongoing support to the beginning teacher. Peer buddies can simply be other faculty members who are within the same grade level or content area as the beginning teacher or who are even just in close proximity to the beginning teacher's classroom.

The peer buddy's role may include supporting the beginning teacher in the following ways:

- Provide quality lessons for observation
- Model appropriate professionalism
- Demonstrate appropriate contact with parents
- Listen and be supportive
- Provide encouragement
- Provide feedback and other ideas and methods of instruction
- Provide resources
- Show examples of lessons
- Share lesson plans and resources

A peer buddy may have concerns when working with the beginning teacher as to how to initially assist and collaborate with members of the collaboration team. To address areas of concern for the peer buddy when implementing a mentoring program it is suggested to use Hall and Hord's Stages of Concern (2006). On the following pages are the stages of concern for the mentor in the order in which they are to be presented:

Stage 0—Awareness Concerns

- If possible, involve peer buddies in discussions and decisions about the innovation and its implementation.
- Share enough information to arouse interest, but not so much that it overwhelms.
- Acknowledge that a lack of awareness is expected and reasonable, and that no questions about the innovation are foolish.
- Encourage unaware persons to talk with colleagues who know about the innovation.
- Take steps to minimize gossip and inaccurate sharing of information about the innovation.

Stage 1—Informational Concerns

- Provide clear and accurate information about the peer buddy process and expectations of the peer buddy.
- Use a variety of ways to share information—verbally, in writing, and through any available media. Communicate with peer buddies and with small and large groups.
- Have persons who have used the innovation in other settings visit with your teachers. Visits to other schools can also be arranged.
- Help peer buddies see how the innovation relates to their current practices, both in regard to similarities and differences.
- Be enthusiastic and enhance the visibility of others who are excited.

Stage 2—Personal Concerns

- Legitimize the existence and expression of peer buddies' personal concerns. Knowing these concerns are common and that others have them can be comforting.
- Use personal notes and conversations to provide encouragement and reinforce personal adequacy.
- Connect peer buddies with other peer buddies across the school district whose personal concerns have diminished and who will be supportive.
- Show how the innovation can be implemented sequentially rather than in one big leap. It is important to establish expectations that are attainable.
- Do not push innovation use, but encourage and support it while maintaining expectations.

Stage 3—Management Concerns

- Clarify the steps and components of the peer buddy process and expectations. Information from innovation configurations will be helpful here.
- Provide answers that address the small and specific "how-to" issues that are so often the cause of management concerns.
- Demonstrate exact and practical solutions to the logistical problems that contribute to the concerns.
- Help teachers sequence specific activities and set timelines for their accomplishments.
- Attend to the immediate demands of the innovation, not what will be or can be in the future.

Stage 4—Consequence Concerns

- Provide peer buddies with opportunities to visit other mentoring settings where the innovation is in use and to attend conferences on the topic.
- Don't overlook these peer buddies. Provide them with positive feedback and needed support.
- Find opportunities for the peer buddies to share their skills with other mentors and other teachers in the profession.
- Share with these peer buddies information pertaining to the innovation.

Stage 5—Collaborative Concerns

- Provide peer buddies with opportunities to develop those skills necessary for working collaboratively.
- Bring together peer buddies, both within and outside the school, who are interested in collaboration.
- Help these peer buddy collaborators establish reasonable expectations and deadlines for the collaborative effort.
- Use these persons to provide technical assistance to others who need assistance.
- Encourage the collaborators, but don't attempt to force collaboration on those mentors who are not interested.

Stage 6—Refocusing Concerns

- Respect and encourage the interest these peer buddies have for finding a better way.

- Help peer buddies channel their ideas and energies in ways that will be productive rather than counterproductive.
- Encourage peer buddies to act on their concerns for program improvement.
- Help peer buddies access resources they may need to refine their ideas and put them into practice.

CONCERN OF KNOWLEDGE OF CURRICULUM, CLASSROOM MANAGEMENT, AND SERVING AS A TEACHER IN THE PROFESSION

Awareness Concerns

Peer buddies express general concern upon receiving their new mentoring assignment with only their knowledge of their own subject matter. Peer buddies need to be given access to resources and trainings that can provide information concerning curriculum as well as classroom management for them to learn in order to best support the beginning teacher.

Peer buddies are given access to the state standards as well as both online and hard copies of curriculum resources. These materials and resources are readily accessible. Peer buddies may be overwhelmed with this new task, but are provided with time and resources to become knowledgeable of the curriculum and information. Support from other peer buddies within a network is established during this time.

Peer buddies have concerns with the beginning teacher's methods of classroom management. Peer buddies are given resources and training on how to assist and support beginning teachers in the areas of classroom discipline, management, routines, and procedures that are aligned with the school-wide rules and philosophy. Peer buddies provide the beginning teacher with examples of rules, routines, and procedures for him or her to reference as he or she creates a classroom management plan.

Peer buddies express concern for the general expectations of them as peer buddies and as contributors to the profession. Peer buddies need to be given clear definitions and roles to refer to in order to adjust to the expectations of the role as a peer buddy. Peer buddies are provided opportunities to engage in conversations with other educators teaching and mentoring at the school or within the district to help clearly define the roles for the beginning teacher in the classroom as well as in the profession.

Informational Concerns

Group discussions about the curriculum among the peer buddies within the same grade or subject levels are initiated. Technological resources are provided as well as other materials of the content knowledge. The information is presented in an enthusiastic manner and is not intended to overwhelm the peer buddies.

Sharing through group discussions about classroom management among the peer buddies within the same grade level or school site is initiated. Peer buddies visit other teachers' classrooms at the school site and at other schools that have mentoring programs and peer buddies established within the same grade level or subject area to observe how various classrooms are managed and how discipline and routines are established in order to best inform the beginning teacher.

Group discussions regarding roles of the peer buddy within the climate of the school are initiated among other peer buddies within the same grade or subject level. The information or written description of the peer buddy's role at the school site is presented to the peer buddy in an enthusiastic manner and is not intended to overwhelm them. The peer buddy is provided with a copy of his or her role and is encouraged to ask questions and discuss the specifics of job duties on a daily basis. The peer buddy is given resources for professional development opportunities throughout the school year as a means for furthering his or her mentor training and education.

Personal Concerns

Peer buddies express personal concern of the unknown. These teachers need to feel validated for their concerns and be able to communicate their needs and wants directly. The administration and collaboration team show that they are available to assist the peer buddy with his or her needs throughout the day and school year. The peer buddy is provided with a risk-free environment to ask for assistance and support from other faculty and administrative members.

Some key areas that peer buddies need clarification in include assisting the new teacher with parent-teacher conferences; special education referrals; duty at recess, before and after school, and at lunchtime; monitoring students in the hallway; determining misbehavior of students; and the teacher's role during the discipline process. The peer buddy is provided with a risk-free environment to ask for assistance and support from other faculty members and fellow mentors when discussing these and other topics.

Peer buddies express concern as to how they can go about training and being involved in mentor professional development as well as how to report back to the faculty what they learned during the training. Peer buddies express questions and interest in returning back to school to achieve a higher degree but are unsure of the expectations of the peer buddy and how much time would be available for higher education.

Management Concerns

The first step in assisting the peer buddy with the curriculum and content knowledge is to provide access to resources and materials needed to plan quality lessons. A laptop or computer is provided for research and instruction in addition to hard copies and online versions of instructional guides, curriculum, and teacher resources. The peer buddy is knowledgeable of the components of the school's or district's lesson plan and any deadlines for submission.

When assisting the beginning teacher with the most effective classroom management methods, the peer buddy is to be provided with access to videos, copies of other management plans, and also school and district handbooks for students so that they are on the same page as beginning teachers. The peer buddy must first have access to these materials and resources in order to gain knowledge of the information he or she will be providing the beginning teacher.

Consequence Concerns

Peer buddies are given release time to observe the classrooms of the beginning teachers that they are supporting as well as to observe other peer buddies within their subject or grade level to gain ideas and information as to different approaches in instruction. These peer buddies are given time to share their new ideas with other peer buddies in their grade level or department within the school or district.

Collaborative Concerns

Peer buddies are given opportunities to attend trainings and professional development within their grade level or content areas. Peer buddies are invited but not required to collaborate with coaches and trainers on a regular basis to reinforce support for the beginning teacher.

Refocusing Concerns

Some peer buddies come to the job with the idea that they already know where the best information is and how to best support the beginning teachers in their school. The administration and collaboration team encourage the peer buddies to express concerns regarding the content knowledge in discussions with other mentors. Peer buddies are provided with opportunities to share their own knowledge of the content and how to best support and exemplify appropriate planning and implementation of instructional practices for the beginning teacher.

KEY POINTS

Chapter eight aligns CBAM with addressing concerns for the peer buddy as he or she becomes involved within a mentoring program. This chapter addresses the peer buddy's concerns about modeling use of curriculum and the professional role of the peer buddy both at the school and within the profession. This chapter explains how to address the concerns and needs a peer buddy may experience as he or she assists the new teacher within a mentoring program.

Chapter Nine

Professional Development Resources

Through the course of a mentoring program, the administration and collaboration team, including the mentor, curriculum coach, and peer buddy, determine best choices for professional development depending on the needs of the first-year teacher. Some possible professional development topics for beginning teachers are outlined in this chapter. One consistent area of professional development need for beginning teachers centers around classroom management.

This chapter contains several professional development topics for beginning teachers but focuses on classroom management as a key need. For the first time in their brand new careers, beginning teachers are provided an empty classroom and a roll sheet of 20 or more students to prepare for on the first day of school. Beginning teachers may not have previously given consideration to their own personal philosophy of classroom management. They may not have ever been asked to create a set of classroom rules, procedures, or consequences for students they will teach.

Before beginning teachers can welcome their new students, there are several things that they must consider to ensure a smooth-running classroom. New teachers struggle with determining which rules, procedures, and consequences are necessary to put into place to begin to establish a safe classroom that encourages a strong rapport among teacher and students. Here is a list of possible professional development topics for beginning teachers:

- Classroom management

  - Procedures
  - Classroom rules
  - Classroom consequences

- Setting up the classroom

- Instructional planning and strategies

  - Curriculum
  - Subject matter
  - Grade-level planning

- Parental conferencing and contact

  - Conferences
  - Involving parents in the classroom
  - Making contact with parents before school starts
  - Continuous feedback on student progress—graded folders weekly

- Time management

  - Creating a schedule
  - Using time wisely during breaks to plan and attend to teacher tasks

- Assessments

  - Informal
  - Formal
  - Standardized

- Special education students

  - Teachers' rights
  - Students' rights
  - Parents' rights

- Continuing education—state professional development requirements, working toward an advanced degree or certification, etc.
- Support from administration—open door policy, frequent observations, and feedback provided
- Paperwork management and filing system

CLASSROOM MANAGEMENT—PROCEDURES

A smooth-running classroom has procedures put into place so that the students are aware of expectations. A teacher with procedures implemented within his or her classroom minimizes distractions and maximizes instructional time.

Example of a procedure:
Entering the room at the beginning of the day
Students are to enter the room quietly. Student homework or folders are to be placed on the upper right-hand corner of the teacher's desk. Students will be seated and begin the assignment on the board at the opening bell.

Other procedures to consider establishing:

1. Whole class attention, quieting the class, or callbacks
2. Collecting papers
3. Taking attendance
4. Broken pencils/sharpening pencils
5. Students needing help during seatwork
6. Restroom privileges
7. Procedures as to when to get out of seat
8. No textbook, paper, pencil, etc.
9. Dismissing class to recess, lunch, end of day, etc.
10. Accessing Chromebooks, iPads, and technology and returning them daily

Classroom Rules

A teacher who sets expectations and aligns consequences for both positive and negative behavior allows students to work within a productive learning environment. Beginning teachers determine three to five classroom rules that align with the school rules while helping to keep students safe and maximize instructional time. Rules are focused on the positive, and negative words such as *not*, *no*, and *never* are avoided.

Examples of classroom rules:

1. I will come to class with all my needed homework, papers, and supplies daily.
2. I will keep my hands and feet to myself.
3. I will respect my classmates' and my teacher's property.

Classroom Consequences

A teacher sets nonpunitive consequences that match the rules of the class. Beginning teachers consider what they will use. The beginning teacher should explain what will be used and be creative! Beginning teachers should become familiar with using positive language when working with students. According to Denton (2014), teachers should use reinforcing, reminding, and redirecting language when working with students. Teachers reinforce the rules and procedures that have been established in the classroom. Teachers remind students of the rules and procedures when students may be getting off track and beginning to exhibit behavior that goes against the rules of the classroom. Teachers should also redirect students' behavior when behaviors continue to go against the rules of the classroom in an effort to maintain the safety and productivity of all students.

Setting Up the Classroom

The classroom is organized for the easy flow of traffic. The desks or tables allow students to see and be seen in their space. The students are able to see the teacher and the area of instructional delivery at all times. The teacher is mindful of where he or she places bookshelves, cubbyholes, textbooks, and other teaching materials to maximize visibility. Bulletin boards and walls have useful information posted but are not so busy that the students become distracted.

INSTRUCTIONAL PLANNING AND STRATEGIES—CURRICULUM

The teacher is knowledgeable of the curriculum being taught. The teacher becomes familiar with specific instructional planning techniques used at the school site along with instructional strategies used to deliver the curriculum. The teacher is provided with textbooks, teacher's manuals, online access to curriculum, and any other resources and materials necessary to become knowledgeable of the content being taught.

Subject Matter

The teacher is able to understand the subject matter being taught. The teacher is able to deliver subject matter that is relevant and meaningful to the students in his or her classroom. The teacher is able to access materials that are content specific and aligned with subject matter being presented.

Grade-Level Planning

The teacher is involved in grade-level planning so as to see what other methods are being used in various classrooms across the grade at the school site. The teacher sits with other members of the grade level and discusses which methods work best with the students at the school when presenting the material.

PARENTAL CONFERENCING AND CONTACT

Teachers make contact with the parents of their students within the first few weeks of the school year. Teachers invite parents to become involved in the school as well as the classroom of their child.

Conferences

Teachers invite parents to come for regular parent-teacher conferences throughout the school year as a means to inform parents of their child's progress. Conferences are scheduled at a time when it is most convenient to both the parent and the teacher. Conferences are scheduled before or after the school day in the classroom or office area.

Involving Parents in the Classroom

Parents are made to feel welcome in the teacher's classroom. Teachers display and model an open door policy provided that the administration and office allow such visitation at appropriate times throughout the school year. Parents are invited to the classroom for presentations, holiday events, and other activities. Parents are invited to the classroom to observe their children if there are areas of concern to be discussed.

Making Contact with Parents before School Starts

Prior to the start of the school year, teachers phone or email parents to welcome their children to the classroom and provide parents with information as to the exciting opportunities that the year will hold for their children. It is the responsibility of the teacher to provide ongoing conversations with the parents of their students as a means of engaging family in the classroom community.

Continuous Feedback on Student Progress—Graded Folders Weekly

Teachers provide continuous feedback to parents regarding student progress. Teachers prepare to send home weekly graded papers in a folder to be signed by the parent. Parents expect to see the ongoing progress of their children. Teachers plan to send home progress reports at specific points throughout the school year as well as report cards at designated times.

TIME MANAGEMENT

Teachers consider time management very carefully when planning their school day. Teachers consider transitions and how long it may take to enter the classroom, have bathroom breaks, complete assignments, change classes, move on to the next subject or activity, and complete other procedures throughout the day.

Creating a Schedule

Teachers create their daily schedule based on the required list of minutes per subject being taught in that specific grade level as set forth by the school administration, district, and state. Teachers consider time for recess, bathroom breaks, lunch, dismissal, and exiting the classroom. The teacher creates a schedule that maximizes instructional time with considerations for student movement and transitions.

Using Time Wisely during Breaks to Plan and Attend to Teacher Tasks

Teachers typically have a 30- to 60-minute break or planning period daily or weekly. During this time the teacher maximizes his or her time wisely and attends to some of the necessary daily duties and paperwork. The teacher plans each day to either prepare for the next lesson during this break time or score or grade assignments that were submitted. This allows the teacher to stay on target with providing feedback in a timely manner and to keep the classroom organized and running smoothly.

ASSESSMENTS

Teachers align their instruction with any assessments given. Teachers plan to assess what is being taught both informally and formally throughout the course of the school year.

Informal

Informal assessments are ongoing assessments that the teacher gives to check for understanding and progress to monitor students. Informal assessments guide instruction and help to let the teacher know where the students are in need of assistance and where they are showing strengths.

Formal

Formal assessments are assessments given at the end of a unit or chapter to summarize what has been taught and learned. These are done independently by the student to measure his or her progress.

Standardized

Standardized assessments are assessments given periodically throughout the school year as a means to see the levels of achievement by each child, teacher's classroom, grade level, school, district, and state. These standardized assessments can be used to measure growth and deficits among students. It is another piece of the achievement report used to determine if students are meeting both curriculum and grade-level expectations deemed typical for that specific grade.

SPECIAL EDUCATION STUDENTS

Today's classroom teacher encounters students with all types of learning exceptionalities. Some students will have special education needs. Teachers of these students are knowledgeable of special education laws, parents' and students' rights, and teachers' rights. Teachers with special education students are familiar with individualized education plans (IEPs) and the implementation of accommodations and modifications.

Teachers' Rights

Teachers have rights when it comes to special education laws and best instructional and professional practices. Teachers are provided with information on any special education child that is in their classroom. Any paperwork or information regarding any accommodations or modifications required for that special education student is provided to the teacher. This paperwork or plan is called an IEP, and the teacher provides services as outlined in the plan.

Students' Rights

Students receiving special education have rights protected by special education laws. Students with identified disabilities will have an IEP, which outlines services that are to be provided. These services include any accommodations or modifications necessary to help the child have success within the classroom environment.

Parents' Rights

The parents of special education students have rights protected by special education laws. Parents of students with an IEP must be invited to conferences and provided time for consent and discussion of the individual education plan prior to implementation. Parents must be notified of any changes made to the IEP. Parents also have full authority to request a meeting during the school year to revisit the IEP or make any suggestions or adjustments.

CONTINUING EDUCATION—STATE PROFESSIONAL DEVELOPMENT REQUIREMENTS, WORKING TOWARD AN ADVANCED DEGREE OR CERTIFICATION, ETC.

Teachers are encouraged to consider continuing education opportunities such as ongoing continuing education courses both online and in person at the district, state, or national level. Teachers also consider furthering their degree path or education by obtaining a master's degree or add-on certification to become better trained in a specific area of interest or need within the profession. By continuing to educate and train themselves on the newest and most innovative methods of instruction, educators take their students to the next level with the most effective teaching methods that allow students to achieve greater gains in their classroom.

SUPPORT FROM ADMINISTRATION—OPEN DOOR POLICY, FREQUENT OBSERVATIONS, AND FEEDBACK PROVIDED

Teachers need support from the administration throughout the school year. In a profession that models appropriate and timely feedback, a teacher also requires such feedback from his or her administrators. Administrators observe teachers on a regular basis and provide ongoing support and feedback as to what is going well and which areas of instruction may need improvement. Administrators should implement a welcoming policy so teachers feel comfortable sharing their experiences and seek advice when needed.

PAPERWORK MANAGEMENT AND FILING SYSTEM

Teachers create a method of managing incoming and outgoing paperwork due to parents as well as to faculty and other administrators. Teachers have a well-organized filing system and desk area that is conducive to completing assignments and paperwork as well as a place for filing graded papers and other data reporting throughout the year.

KEY POINTS

Chapter nine provides several professional development resources aimed at enhancing the new teacher's repertoire of skills within their first year. Here a full list of suitable topics based on the concerns of new teachers is outlined. The mentor teacher, curriculum coach, peer buddy, and administrators may choose to deliver any or all of these professional development topics to the new teacher throughout the first year of teaching. Special attention is given to classroom management as this seems to be an area of greatest concern when working with new teachers.

Chapter Ten

Beginning Teacher Retreat and Induction

Just before the start of the school year, it is recommended that beginning teachers attend a retreat. At this retreat, sessions in various areas of classroom management and instructional practices are provided. This could be an overnight retreat at a location agreed on by faculty or simply a day retreat, perhaps on a weekend.

The retreat is initially for beginning teachers, and veteran teachers are invited to provide learning sessions on valuable topics such as classroom management, organization, curriculum alignment, integrating technology, state standards, and basic paperwork handling within the school. At the retreat, the beginning teachers are introduced to their individual collaboration teams and reflect on how the ideas they learn about can be implemented in their classrooms. Some topics for the retreat may include the following:

- duties of the teacher
- roles of the teacher, mentor, peer buddy, and coach
- dress code
- code of ethics
- chain of command
- schedule
- duty
- school rules
- mailboxes
- paperwork
- creating a classroom management plan
- parent–teacher communication
- calculating grades

- grading scale and sending home progress reports
- insurance
- schoolwide discipline procedures
- special education forms and referrals
- special education accommodations and interventions
- teacher parking
- teacher insurance, salary schedule, pay periods
- holidays
- other key areas of importance

Beginning teachers participating in a mentoring program attend an induction to be held prior to the start of the school year to meet the administration, mentors, collaboration team members, as well as other faculty. The beginning teachers are given school information, a copy of the actual evaluation form that will be used to assess the beginning teacher throughout the year, and quality lesson plans or videos of highly effective lessons to refer to as examples in preparation for the initial evaluation.

During this induction, the beginning teachers come to understand the process that will be put into place to help assist them to be successful throughout their first three years of teaching. They are assigned their mentor, coach, and peer buddy to assist them through the process. The administration schedules the first formal observation of the beginning teacher in the classroom within the first quarter of the school year.

The induction should be held during a workday prior to the beginning of the school year. This is a time when the beginning teacher becomes familiar with such topics as classroom management, beginning of the year paperwork, schoolwide rules and procedures, instructional strategies and evaluations, policies involving parental involvement and communication, daily class schedules, curriculum, lesson planning requirements, instructional strategies, school policies on integrating technology, homework, assessments, special education students, and provided support from the administration.

An example list of beginning teacher induction points of interest are as follows:

- setting classroom and personal/professional goals
- teacher evaluation system
- collaboration with peer buddies, mentors, coaches, and administration
- establishing a classroom management plan
- providing immediate parental feedback
- school's calendar of events
- plan for individual professional development

SCHEDULE EXAMPLE OF A TWO-DAY INDUCTION PROGRAM

Day One—New Teacher Induction

8:00–8:30	greeting and icebreaker (coach)
8:30–9:00	introductions of mentor, coach, and peer buddy (members of collaboration team)
9:00–10:00	district and school policies and procedures (administrator)
10:00–10:15	break
10:15–11:15	school-level expectations of teachers and additional duties (peer buddy)
11:15–12:30	lunch
12:30–1:30	classroom rules, procedures, and consequences (mentor)
1:30–2:30	school calendar, classroom schedule, additional classes (coach)
2:30–3:00	reflection, followed by a survey if needed

Day Two—New Teacher Induction

8:00–8:30	greeting and icebreaker (coach)
8:30–9:00	paperwork and organization (administration)
9:00–10:00	special education information and procedures/laws (special education contact)
10:00–10:15	break
10:15–11:15	curriculum and subject matter by grade level (breakout session by grade level)
11:15–12:30	lunch
12:30–1:30	teacher evaluation and rubric used (mentor)
1:30–2:30	setting professional goals and professional development
2:30–3:00	reflection

KEY POINTS

Chapter ten provides the administrator with suggestions for organizing a new teacher retreat and induction program for beginning teachers. This chapter gives examples of key topics to be addressed at both a retreat and an induction when implementing a mentoring program. The chapter also provides a model two-day induction schedule that addresses these key topics in partnership with the whole collaboration team.

Chapter Eleven

Guiding and Documenting Implementation

This book provides four questionnaires for administrators to utilize to measure and track the change process while implementing the mentoring program within the school. These four questionnaires are designed for the administrator to gain information about the implementation of the mentoring program. The administrator can benefit from these questionnaires throughout the implementation process.

Beginning teachers will take the *Beginning Teacher Questionnaire* to determine their needs at the induction period. This is a sort of interest inventory to see what they are most concerned with, and it shows their immediate needs at the time of hiring. This questionnaire is given to beginning teachers prior to the start of the school year and can be used periodically throughout the school year as administrators want to probe and see if new needs surface.

Beginning teachers are given a *Beginning Teacher Exit Survey* within the last two weeks of their first year of the mentoring program. This exit survey serves as a measure of goals that were met or unmet within the program. It provides information that will inform educational leaders and administrators of areas to improve within the school's mentoring program for the next year.

The chapter provides another questionnaire for the members of the collaboration team called the *Collaboration Team Exit Survey*. This survey is designed for the mentor, coach, and peer buddy to take at the end of each year of the mentoring program. The mentor, coach, and peer buddy are allowed the opportunity to provide any suggested changes that they feel should be implemented for the next school year. This questionnaire also gives insight into what worked well for the new teacher from the lens of the mentor, coach, and peer buddy.

The *Experienced Teacher Questionnaire* is the fourth instrument provided in this chapter and is designed for newly experienced teachers who are in their second through fifth years of teaching. This questionnaire will help track those new teachers who have completed their first year at the school and are entering their second year. It will help to target any topics or needs of the teacher that may not have been addressed in the first year of the mentoring program.

BEGINNING TEACHER QUESTIONNAIRE

(To be given to new hires in their first year of teaching, prior to the start of the school year.)

1. Which do you feel is your most valued classroom teaching tool? (Number in order of importance from 1 to 5, 5 being the highest.)

    __computer __teacher books __smartboard __manipulatives __curriculum

2. What are your expectations for your principal?
3. What do you feel the most uneasy about in beginning your first year teaching?
4. What do you feel confident about?
5. What do you feel is the mentor's role?
6. What would you like the coach to do for you?
7. What are your general behavioral expectations for your class?
8. Please rate how you feel about the following statements:

    I feel positive about learning new things.
    ____strongly disagree ____disagree ____agree ____strongly agree
    I feel comfortable sharing new things with a group.
    ____strongly disagree ____disagree ____agree ____strongly agree
    I am not comfortable presenting new ideas to a group.
    ____strongly disagree ____disagree ____agree ____strongly agree
    I would be comfortable facilitating change within a group.
    ____strongly disagree ____disagree ____agree ____strongly agree

9. Rank the following items from 1 to 7 (7 being the highest and 1 being the lowest) based on what you value the most as a teacher:

    ____professional development and training
    ____curriculum and content
    ____classroom discipline
    ____classroom management
    ____parental involvement

____paperwork and teacher duties and roles
____obtaining a higher degree (master's, educational specialist, doctorate)

BEGINNING TEACHER EXIT SURVEY

(To be given to the beginning teacher at the close of his or her first school year.)

1. During this year, what was your most valued classroom tool?
2. During this year, what did you feel you needed the most assistance with?
3. What was the most important area of training that was given to you this past year?
4. What was the most challenging for you during your first year of teaching?
5. If you could give a beginning teacher at this school or in the profession any advice, what would it be and why?
6. What is one thing that you felt unclear about at the beginning of the school year?
7. How can the mentor better meet your needs?
8. How can the coach better meet your needs?
9. What is one recommendation that can help to improve the beginning teacher program and collaboration team as a whole?
10. How did you initially feel about coming from college to the classroom? (Rate from 1 to 5, 5 being the highest.)

    ___very unprepared ___unprepared ___adequately prepared ___prepared ___very prepared

11. How do you feel about continuing in the profession?

    ___very unprepared ___unprepared ___adequately prepared ___prepared ___very prepared

COLLABORATION TEAM EXIT SURVEY

(To be given to the teachers at the school site who serve as mentors, coaches, or peer buddies within a mentoring program at the school.)

1. Over this past year of teaching, what was your most valued classroom tool?
2. Over this past year of teaching, what did you feel you needed most but didn't have?

3. Rank the following from 1 to 6 in order of training/professional development importance to you as a teacher:

   ____professional development
   ____curriculum alignment
   ____classroom management
   ____parental involvement training
   ____paperwork and teacher duties and roles
   ____obtaining a higher degree (master's)

4. What was the most important thing that you feel your mentee benefitted from learning from you this year?
5. What was the most challenging aspect of the mentoring process this year?
6. If you could give a beginning teacher at this school or in the profession any advice, what would it be and why?
7. What is one thing that you think should change about the mentoring program for next year?

EXPERIENCED TEACHER QUESTIONNAIRE

(To be given to the teachers at the school site who are in their second through fifth years of teaching at the school.)

1. In your first year teaching, what was your most valued classroom tool?
2. In your first year teaching, what did you feel you needed most but didn't have?
3. Rank the following from 1 to 6 in order of training/professional development importance to you as a teacher:

   ____professional development
   ____curriculum alignment
   ____classroom management
   ____parental involvement training
   ____paperwork and teacher duties and roles
   ____obtaining a higher degree (master's)

4. What was the most important aspect that someone helped you with in your first year teaching?
5. What was the most challenging for you during the first year teaching?
6. If you could give a beginning teacher at your school or in the profession any advice, what would it be and why?
7. What is one thing that you felt unclear about starting at a new school and in a new job?

KEY POINTS

Chapter eleven provides information for guiding and documenting the implementation of the mentoring program within a school. This chapter provides four questionnaires/surveys that administrators can use to collect data and determine any improvements and changes that are to be made during implementation. They include the Beginning Teacher Questionnaire, Beginning Teacher Exit Survey, Collaboration Team Exit Survey, and Experienced Teacher Questionnaire.

Chapter Twelve

Timeline of Implementation

Chapter twelve provides a detailed timeline that will help make this mentoring program effective. This is known as the *Timeline of Mentoring Program Implementation* and provides a detailed account of the administrator's duties throughout the first year of the program, as well as a month-by-month list of duties of all within the collaboration team. The timeline of implementation addresses the responsibilities that the collaboration team has to each other as well as to the mentee or new teacher. Finally, the timeline suggests dates for formal observations of the new teacher by the team as well as when to establish and adjust the new teacher's professional teaching goals. There is also the *Timeline of Progression from Mentee to Mentor*, which takes the mentee through the process of becoming a peer buddy, coach, and mentor.

These timelines are designed to be implemented within the first few weeks of beginning the mentoring program.

KEY POINTS

This chapter provides two timelines for that will help make the mentoring program effective. The *Timeline of Mentoring Program Implementation* details the duties throughout the first year for the administrator, mentor teacher, coach, and peer buddy. The *Timeline of Progression from Mentee to Mentor* is provided to show the appropriate phases one must go through to become a mentor after initially being a mentee.

Table 12.1. *Timeline of Mentoring Program Implementation*

Month	Administrator duties	Collaboration team duties
1	Beginning teacher retreat, induction; administer the questionnaire Beginning Teacher Questionnaire; provide digital copies of the beginning teacher training books for everyone involved; assign mentors, coaches, and peer buddies.	Attend beginning teacher retreat, induction; read and become familiar with the mentoring books.
2	Set up collaboration teams; assign locations; plan and hold first formal observation.	Hold first collaboration team meeting with new teacher; prepare him or her for first formal observation.
3	Continually meet as a collaboration team; adjust goals; provide professional development.	Continually meet as a collaboration team; adjust goals; provide professional development.
4	Oversee planning for and hold second formal observation by administration.	Hold second collaboration team meeting with new teacher; prepare him or her for second formal observation.
5	Refresh collaboration team on current goals for their new teachers; provide professional development opportunities for the beginning teacher and organize release time.	Attend collaboration team meeting with administrators and adjust and discuss goals for new teachers; work with new teacher to sit with his or her class to allow for professional development; provide some trainings and professional development based on his or her needs.
6	Plan for and hold third formal observation by administration.	Prepare new teacher for third formal observation.
7	Continually meet as a collaboration team, adjust goals, review second formal observation, and conference about improvements needed (if any).	Attend collaboration team meeting with administrators and adjust and discuss goals for new teachers.
8	Plan for and hold fourth formal observation by administration.	Prepare new teacher for fourth formal observation.
9	End of the year conference and placement for the next school year; administer the Beginning Teacher Exit Survey; administer the Collaboration Team Exit Survey; collect surveys and plan for future changes in the program's implementation.	Take the Collaboration Team Exit Survey (for mentors, coaches, and peer buddy teachers).

Table 12.2. Timeline of progression from mentee to mentor

Year	Mentee is given mentoring and coaching support	Peer buddy status	Coach status	Mentor teacher status
1	Y	N	N	N
2	Y	Y	N	N
3	Y	Y	Y	N
4	N	Y	Y	Y
5	N	Y	Y	Y

Y = Yes; N = No

References

Bailey, D. B., & Palsha, S. A. (1992). Qualities of the Stages of Concern Questionnaire and implications for educational innovations. *The Journal of Educational Research, 85*(4), 226–232. http://dx.doi.org/10.1080/00220671.1992.9941120

Christesen, E., & Turner, J. (2014). Identifying teachers attending professional development by their stages of concern: Exploring attitudes and emotions. *Teacher Educator, 49*(4), 232–246. doi:10.1080/08878730.2014.933641

Darling-Hammond, L. (2006). Securing the right to learn: Policy and practice for powerful teaching and learning. *Educational Researcher, 35*(7), 13–24.

Deci, E., Koestner, R., & Ryan, R. (1999). A meta-analytic review of experiments examining the effects of extrinsic rewards on intrinsic motivation. *Psychological Bulletin, 125*(6), 627–668. http://home.ubalt.edu/tmitch/642/Articles%20syllabus/Deci%20Koestner%20Ryan%20meta%20IM%20psy%20bull%2099.pdf

Denton, P. (2014). *The power of our words: Teacher language that helps children learn.* Turners Falls, MA: Northeast Foundation for Children.

Di Carlo, M. (2015). *Update on teacher turnover in the U.S. Shanker Institute.* Retrieved from http://www.shankerinstitute.org/blog/update-teacher-turnover-us

Dudovskiy, J. (2013). *Frederick Hertzberg's two-factory theory: Research methodology.* Retrieved from http://research-methodology.net/frederick-hertzbergs-two-factor-theory/

Fibkins, W. L. (2002). *An administrator's guide to better teacher mentoring.* Lanham, MD: Scarecrow Press.

Frase, L. E. (1989). Effects of teacher rewards on recognition and job enrichment. *Journal of Educational Research, 83*(1), 52–57.

Ganser, T. (1997). *Promises and pitfalls for mentors of beginning teachers.* University of Wisconsin, WI. Diversity in Mentoring Conference, Tempe, AZ.

George, A. A., Hall, G. E., & Stiegelbauer, S. M. (2006). *Measuring implementation in schools: The Stages of Concern Questionnaire.* Austin, TX: SEDL/American Institutes for Research.

Hall, G., & Hord, S. (2006). *Implementing change: Patterns, principles and potholes.* Boston, MA: Pearson.

Herzberg, F. (1959). *The motivation to work.* New York, NY: Wiley.

Herzberg, F. (1966). *Work and the nature of man.* New York, NY. Thomas Y. Crowell.

Hord, S. M., Rutherford, W. L., Huling-Austin, L., & Hall, G. E. (1987). *Taking charge of change.* Alexandria, VA: ASCD.

Huling, L., & Resta, V. (2001). *Teacher mentoring as professional development.* Washington, DC: ERIC Clearinghouse on Teaching and Teacher Education. Retrieved from ERIC database. (ED460125)

Ingersoll, R. M. (2012). Beginning teacher induction: What the data tell us. *Phi Delta Kappa International, 93*(8), 47–51.

Ingersoll, R., & Merrill, L. (2010). Who's teaching our children? *Educational Leadership, 67*(8), 14–20.

Ingersoll, R. M., & Smith, T. M. (2003). The wrong solution to the teacher shortage. *Educational Leadership, 60*(8), 30–33.

Knight, J. (2007). *Instructional coaching: A partnership approach to improving instruction.* Thousand Oaks, CA: Corwin.

Kochran, F. K., & Smith, S. B. (2000). From mentoring to co-mentoring: Establishing collaborative relationships. *Theory into Practice, 39*(1), 20–28.

Maslow, A. H. (1943). A theory of human motivation. *Psychological Review, 50*(4), 370–396.

Olson, R. M. (2008). *Mentoring as a source of growth for mentors* (Doctoral dissertation). Retrieved from ProQuest. (3343542)

Perrachione, B. A., Rosser, V. J., & Petersen, G. J. (2008). Why do they stay? Elementary teachers' perceptions of job satisfaction and retention. *The Professional Educator, 32*(2).

Robbins, P. (1991). *How to plan and implement a peer coaching program.* ASCD. Retrieved from http://www.ascd.org/publications/books/61191149/chapters/A-Definition-of-Peer-Coaching.aspx

Rowley, J. (1999). Supporting new teachers: The good mentor. *Educational Leadership, 56*(8), 20–22.

Saunders, R. R. (2012). Assessment of professional development for teachers in the vocational education and training sector: An examination of the Concerns Based Adoption Model. *Australian Journal of Education, 56*(2), 182–204.

Sorbet, S. (2018). *Mentoring: Who really grows? An examination of the reciprocity between a mentor and a new teacher* (Doctoral dissertation). Retrieved from ProQuest. (10831074)

Stello, C. M. (2011). *Herzberg's two-factor theory of job satisfaction: An Integrative Literature Review.* University of Minnesota, MN. Retrieved from http//: www.cehd.umn.edu/01opd/research/student conf/2011

About the Authors

Stefanie R. Sorbet, EdD, is an assistant professor at the University of Central Arkansas (UCA) in the Department of Elementary, Literacy, and Special Education. Dr. Sorbet began her career of over 18 years as an elementary teacher in Louisiana within the Tangipahoa Parish public school system, serving rural, at-risk students. She began mentoring preservice teachers. Dr. Sorbet later served as an instructor at Southeastern Louisiana University, where she mentored and supported elementary education preservice teachers in literacy and classroom management courses as well as field placements. During this time she worked extensively in partnership with Louisiana public school districts, fostering relationships between mentors and preservice teachers; provided professional development training; and supported new teachers as they transitioned into their first year of teaching.

Dr. Sorbet's research interests include mentoring to improve new teacher retention and the necessity of authentic experiences prior to their first year of teaching. She is the author of *Mentoring: Who Grows? An Examination of the Reciprocity between a Mentor and a New Teacher*. She has also published articles on the importance of role play in the college classroom as a method of providing authentic pre-practicum experiences.

She served most recently as the secretary of the Louisiana Education Research Association (LERA). Dr. Sorbet instructs elementary education majors at UCA in such courses as positive classroom environment and guidance and management of children. She currently resides in Arkansas with her husband, Gregory; daughters, Sydney and Ryan; and son, Owen.

Patricia Kohler-Evans, EdD, is a professor at the University of Central Arkansas in the Department of Elementary, Literacy, and Special Education. As a former teacher, she has worked with students with disabilities for over 30 years. She has 19 years of experience as a special education administrator in the largest district in Arkansas, serving urban students with numerous needs stemming from poverty, disability, and race. While there, she focused on inclusive education and making sure that the needs of all students were met. During her tenure in Little Rock, the district cohosted the state's first conference on inclusive education.

Dr. Kohler-Evans's research interests include inclusive education and meeting the needs of all students in various settings. She is the coauthor of *Civility, Compassion, and Courage in Schools Today: Strategies for Implementing in K–12 Schools*, *Success Favors Well-Prepared Teachers: Devel-*

oping Routines and Relationships to Improve School Culture, and *Meaningful Conversations: The Way to Comprehensive and Transformative School Improvement*. She has also published numerous articles on coteaching and the importance of developing positive relationships with students as well as teachers.

She serves as an executive coach for the Little Rock School District. Dr. Kohler-Evans is also director of the UCA Mashburn Center for Learning, a center devoted to providing K–12 teachers with tools they need for teaching in diverse school settings.

www.ingramcontent.com/pod-product-compliance
Lightning Source LLC
Chambersburg PA
CBHW021847220426
43663CB00005B/433